THE NEGOTIATION HANDBOOK

Negotiation is an essential skill for all those operating commercially on behalf of their organisations. The ability to negotiate quotations, tenders, proposals, internal and external stakeholders, licensing agreements and so on, could form a critical part of any employee's role, be it on the buy or supply side.

The Negotiation Handbook is a useful guide for all those wanting to understand how to apply tools and techniques to the negotiation process. This handbook has been subdivided into seven key sections, each representing a key phase in the negotiation process. The models and concepts are presented so that both a pictorial and explanatory commentary is available to the reader.

This practical handbook supports all those working in a commercial capacity, so that they may apply commonly used tools and techniques and gain maximum benefit on behalf of their employers.

Andrea Cordell is a well-known international speaker and author on strategy, negotiation and procurement-related matters. She has worked in senior positions at several global organisations and is currently the managing director of Cordie Ltd, a leading sales and procurement training and consulting company.

T0384231

THE NEGOTIATION HANDBOOK

Second Edition

Andrea Cordell

LONDON AND NEW YORK

Second edition published 2019
by Routledge
2 Park Square, Milton Park, Abingdon, Oxon, OX14 4RN

and by Routledge
711 Third Avenue, New York, NY 10017

Routledge is an imprint of the Taylor & Francis Group, an informa business

First edition published by Chartered Institute of Purchasing & Supply 2014

British Library Cataloguing-in-Publication Data
A catalogue record for this book is available from the British Library

Library of Congress Cataloging-in-Publication Data
A catalog record has been requested for this book

ISBN: 978-0-8153-7555-5 (hbk)
ISBN: 978-0-8153-7554-8 (pbk)
ISBN: 978-1-351-23954-7 (ebk)

Typeset in Bembo
by Apex CoVantage, LLC

CONTENTS

FIGURES

TEMPLATES

ACKNOWLEDGEMENTS

To all those who have helped with the development of this book.

A special mention to: Professor Malcolm Higgs at Southampton University who coached me through my doctoral research on negotiation, Ian Thompson and Tracey Webster at Cordie for their critical input and Samantha Wheeler, for her editing skills.

INTRODUCTION

Negotiation is regarded as a key skill for those operating in the business environment.

This book is aimed at helping those wishing to increase negotiation capability whether it is for application in the workplace, for personal use or for students who are pursuing examinations. Replicating the style of the hugely popular *The Procurement Models Handbook*, it provides both students and business managers with a simple analysis of the most common models and concepts associated with the negotiation process.

It is hoped that both students and practitioners alike will find it a quick and effective source of reference prior to planning that all-important negotiation.

The negotiation process

There are many versions of the negotiation process in existence, but perhaps the most well-known and enduring version is that by Professor Leonard Greenhalgh, published in 2001 and founded upon extensive research.

The model identifies the basic 'process' of negotiation in a linear series of seven sequential steps (see Figure 0.1):

Phase 1. **Preparation** – Deciding what is important, defining goals, thinking ahead how to work together with the other party.

Phase 2. **Relationship building** – Getting to know the other party, understanding how you and the other are similar or different, building commitment toward achieving a mutually beneficial set of outcomes.

Phase 3. **Information gathering** – Learning what you need to know about the issues, the other party and their needs, the feasibility of possible settlements, and what might happen if you fail to reach agreement with the other side.

Phase 4. **Information using** – At this stage, negotiators assemble the case they want to make for their preferred outcomes and settlement, one that will maximise the negotiator's own needs. This presentation is often used to 'sell'

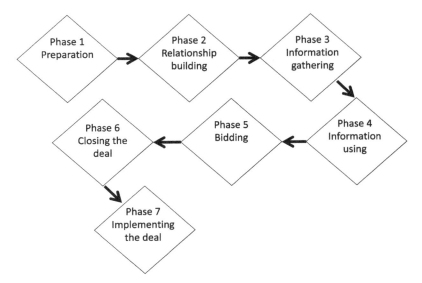

Figure 0.1 The negotiation process

Source: Adapted from Greenhalgh (2001)

the negotiator's preferred outcome to the other.

Phase 5. **Bidding** – The process of making moves from one's initial, ideal position to the actual outcome. Bidding is the process by which each party states their 'opening offer', and then makes moves in that offer toward a middle ground.

Phase 6. **Closing the deal** – The objective here is to build commitment to the agreement achieved in the previous phase. Both the negotiator and the other party have to assure themselves that they reached a deal they can be happy with or, at least, live with.

Phase 7. **Implementing the deal** – Determining who needs to do what once the agreement is formalised. Not uncommonly, parties discover that the agreement has anomalies, key points were missed, or the situation has changed and is sometimes subject to renegotiation.

This book tracks the flow of the Greenhalgh framework and presents readers with a summary of just some of the pre-eminent models and concepts that can be used at each stage.

Choice of models and concepts

In preparing this book, I have reviewed many academic texts/papers/journals and negotiation books by a plethora of different authors. The books appear to have been mostly based on personal opinion and perspective, and have ranged from interesting and light-hearted to the downright wacky.

Therefore, the models and concepts that form the content of this book have been selected wherever possible from research with supporting empirical evidence. Other inclusion criteria are as follows:

- Whether the content can be applied practically in the context of the negotiation process.
- Whether the content is an original concept, rather than a later adaptation.

Each stage of the negotiation process has been assessed by leading academics and practitioners in order to arrive at a consensus.

Presentation of models and concepts

The models and concepts are presented so that both a pictorial and explanatory commentary is available to the reader. The format for each is as follows:

- **Overview** – A brief introduction of the model/concept.
- **Elements** – A description or definition of the key parts of the model/concept.
- **So what?** – A guide as to how the model/concept is generally used in a practical sense in the negotiation process.
- **Negotiation application** – Suggestions as to how the model/concept can be applied specifically in a negotiation context.
- **Limitations** – An open and even-handed critique of the model/concept.
- **Further reading** – A pointer to key works and/or texts on the underpinning theory.
- **Associated template** – An accompanying template and/or additional guidance that could be used by the practitioner, which can be found at the back of the book in the templates and bibliography section.

PHASE 1

Preparation

Overview

It is assumed that considerable strategic analysis will have taken place prior to the commencement of the negotiation process. Many of the models and frameworks discussed in the corresponding text, *The Procurement Models Handbook*, may have been used to assist in the development of the negotiation strategy.

Once the planning process has been completed, ratified, sponsored, and a potential source identified, it is then time to make the deal.

This section focuses on the initial key activities that will help to set the scene for the practical negotiation:

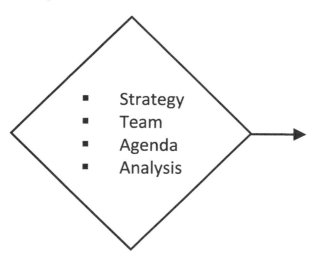

Figure 1.0   Phase 1: Preparation

1

NEGOTIATION STRATEGY

Figure 1.1 Negotiation Strategies Continuum

Overview

Walton and McKersie (1991), first proposed two approaches to negotiation in 1965 when researching industrial relations disputes. This notion was later popularised by Fisher and Ury (1982) in their hugely popular book *Getting to Yes. Negotiating Agreement Without Giving In*. It is now generally accepted that there are essentially two types of negotiation strategy. These are commonly referred to as:

* **Integrative**, also known as collaborative, interest-based or win/win.
* **Distributive**, also known as competitive, position-based or win/lose.

More recently literature has pointed to a third type called 'win/perceived win', which is gaining popularity among academics and practitioners and is viewed as a pragmatic, commercially astute alternative.

Elements

These strategies are often explained in terms of a pie; i.e., sharing it out equally or in some cases making it bigger, aka 'expanding the pie', or conversely cutting up the pie, which means that one party will miss out.

Integrative (win/win)

This involves joint effort directed at finding a solution that will be seen as beneficial to both parties. Parties engaged in integrative negotiations usually recognise that they have common interests and goals and collaborate in order to 'share the pie'. Integrative negotiation is characterised by:

- Cooperation
- Focus on the parties commonalties
- Exchange of information and ideas
- Creating options for mutual gain.

Distributive (win/lose)

This is used when each party focuses on who gets how much of what, and concession will only occur in order to obtain a basic agreement. Each party views the other as an adversary and the objective is to 'obtain as much of the pie' as possible. Distributive negotiation is characterised by:

- Coercion
- Focus on the parties differences
- Power play
- Lack of concessions.

Win/perceived win

This is adopted when one party wants to ensure they 'obtain as much of the pie as possible' but at the same time giving the appearance of 'sharing the pie'. It is argued that this will ensure competitive advantage while also retaining the dynamics required for a long-term relationship.

So what?

Knowing which approach to take when is referred to as the 'negotiator's dilemma', and it is likely that most negotiations will have both distributive and integrative elements, hence the increasing profile of the win/perceived win concept.

It is essential that an appropriate strategy is identified prior to entering into the negotiation, as this will provide the framework for how it will be conducted, the behaviour exhibited and the types of persuasion methods and tactics selected.

Negotiation application

- Provides a framework for the negotiation plan.
- Sets the tone for the negotiation.
- Gives focus to the required outcomes.

Limitations

There is much debate as to which type of negotiation produces the best outcome, and choice is dependent upon circumstances such as market conditions, relationship and type of product/service. It may also be dependent upon the negotiator's personality, with some naturally veering towards one type over another.

Further reading

You can read more about negotiation strategy in:

Fisher, R., Ury, W. and Patton, B. (1982). *Getting to Yes: Negotiating an Agreement Without Giving In*. 1st edition. London: Hutchinson Paperback.
Walton, R.E. and McKersie, R.B. (1991). *A Behavioural Theory of Labor Negotiations: An Analysis of a Social Interaction System*. 2nd edition. Ithaca, NY: Cornell University Press.

Associated template

The following template can be used to develop the negotiation strategy:

• Template 1: Strategy Adoption Matrix.

2

NEGOTIATION TEAM

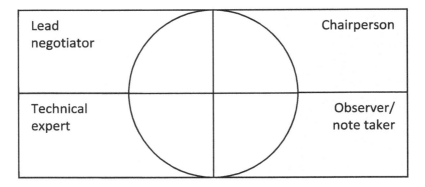

Lead negotiator			Chairperson
Technical expert			Observer/ note taker

Figure 1.2 The negotiation team

Overview

Establishing the team is a critical part of the negotiation process as personalities, skills and role apportionment need to be taken into consideration. It is likely that a number of participants will have been involved in the build-up to the negotiation; however, not everyone can have a seat at the table itself.

Relationships, positioning and differing perspectives among team members can complicate the ways in which the strategy and tactics are used in order to work towards a negotiated settlement. It is therefore important to ensure that all participants understand what their role is and their scope of responsibility.

Elements

Selecting the participant	It is important to assess the skills required, and the strengths and weaknesses of each potential participant. Research suggests that the optimum number for a team negotiation is 3–4; however, this varies depending upon sector and complexity of the negotiation.
Team roles	The three main roles are: ■ Chairperson/lead negotiator ■ Technical expert ■ Observer/note taker The chairperson/lead negotiator role may be split.
Agreeing priorities	It is possible that each participant will have their own list of priorities when it comes to the outcomes. These will need to be agreed within the team as it will inform the negotiation agenda.
Devising a code amongst team members	Prior to the negotiation a code should be devised between the team that allows signals to be sent and received undetected by the other party during the negotiation.
Rules of engagement	The designated lead negotiator should discuss potential tactics that may be used during the negotiation, so that they may be deployed successfully.

Figure 1.3   Elements of the negotiation team

So what?

A study by Thompson, Peterson and Brodt (1996) found that when teams rather than individuals negotiate they are likely to engender an integrative approach. It is thought that this may be due to the increased flow of information between the parties.

Negotiation application

- The negotiation requires a diverse set of knowledge, abilities, or expertise.
- A range of interests must be represented at the table.
- To display a dominant position to the other party.
- To signal to the other side the seriousness of the negotiation.
- To show the depth of relationship among the party.
- Some cultures require that team rather than individuals negotiate.

Limitations

Academics assert that teams in general need to be heterogeneous rather than homogenous in make-up, and that the optimum team number is somewhere between five and seven members. This could suggest that anything outside of these parameters is ineffective, but further research is needed to support such an assertion.

Further reading

You can read more about negotiation teams in:

Thompson, L., Peterson, E. and Brodt, S.E. (1996). Team negotiations: an examination of integrative and distributive bargaining. *Journal of Personality and Social Psychology*, 70, 66–78.

Associated template

The following template can be used to support the development of the negotiation team:

- Template 2: Negotiation Roles

3

NEGOTIATION AGENDA

Negotiation agenda

1) Structure
2) Home or away
3) Room ergonomics
4) Timings
5) Agenda item positioning

Figure 1.4 The negotiation agenda

Overview

Managing the negotiation meeting(s) will involve careful consideration of the various resources required, such as attendees, room layout and timings. Much of this is covered by the agenda, which can be prepared in advance. It may then be used as a checklist and also as a conditioning tool if shared with the other party beforehand.

One of the biggest agenda dilemmas is whether to introduce the 'big ticket' items early on, or to leave them to the end. This may be determined by whether you are negotiating from a buyer or seller perspective.

Elements

Factors that need to be considered when preparing the agenda are:

Structure

A typical negotiation agenda might include the following items:

- Attendees
- Introductions

- Negotiation variables to be discussed
- Breakout
- Review negotiation position
- Summarise negotiation position
- Wrap up and close.

Home or away

This refers to whether the staging of the event takes place on home ground or away at the other party's site. There are advantages and disadvantages to both:

Home advantages:

- Feel confident in home surroundings
- In control of the negotiating environment
- Immediate access to resources such as documentation/IT.

Home disadvantages:

- Inability to access the other party's resources
- Visiting party may feel more pressurised and therefore more defensive.

Away advantages:

- Immediate access to the other party's resources
- Home team likely to feel more comfortable and therefore less defensive.

Away disadvantages:

- Could feel less confident when not on home ground
- Unable to access own resources such as IT, key stakeholders, etc.

Room ergonomics

This refers to room layout and associated detail. One of the key decisions will revolve around the seating plan, i.e., should negotiating parties be facing directly opposite each other or slightly to an angle at the side? This will also be dependent upon the table size, shape and chair arrangement. The availability of refreshments (or not), use of mobile phones, provision of presentation equipment and additional breakout areas will also need to be factored in.

Timings

Some negotiators prefer to leave the negotiation to flow naturally, without time restriction, while others like to have fixed start and end times with predetermined breakout sessions. It should be noted that certain cultures are more monochromic (adherence to time) opposed to polychromic (adherence to relationships rather than time), which could affect how agenda timings are managed.

Agenda item positioning

Academics cannot agree how 'big ticket' (high value) issues/items should be treated. On the one hand it is thought that discussing 'big ticket' items early on can secure a solid foundation from which to build incrementally (popular with buyers); however, the counter to this suggests that by holding back, one can 'wear down' the other party, so that by the end of the process there is very little fight left in the opposing party (popular with sellers). Again, it should be noted that the issue of big versus small may also be affected by culture.

So what?

Structuring a negotiation with an agenda not only provides parameters for those attending, but can also act as a conditioning tool. Setting out in advance who is attending ensures that the parties can match power and authority levels; revealing what items are to be discussed/negotiated helps to set objectives and expectations; and informing those participating of the amount of time and resources to be contributed to the process bestows importance upon the event.

Negotiation application

- Supports the management of the negotiation.
- Helps to provide the right setting for the negotiation.
- Can facilitate the flow of communication between the two parties.
- Supports overall negotiation strategy, i.e., big vs. small.

Limitations

Agendas can act merely as checklists and therefore can be deemed as unnecessary additional administration. Also, there are negotiators who prefer a less formalised approach for a variety of reasons such as personal style, culture of the organisation and effort required in comparison to overall reward.

Further reading

You can read more about negotiation agendas in:

Lysons, K. and Farrington, B. (2012). *Purchasing and Supply Chain Management*. 8th edition. Harlow: Pearson.

Associated template

The following template can be used to support the development of the negotiation agenda:

- Template 3: Negotiation Agenda Checklist

4

NEGOTIATION SWOT ANALYSIS

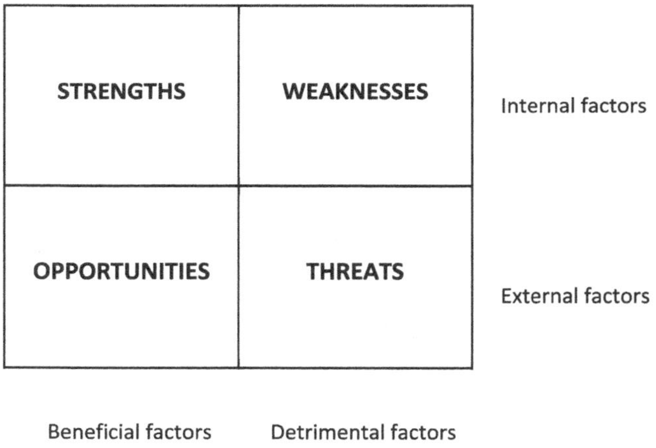

STRENGTHS	WEAKNESSES	Internal factors
OPPORTUNITIES	THREATS	External factors

Beneficial factors   Detrimental factors

Figure 1.5   SWOT

Overview

SWOT analysis emanated from the Stanford Research Institute in the mid-1960s. The model is a mnemonic (for strengths, weaknesses, opportunities and threats) representing the factors for analysis when assessing a business or a proposition. It is a subjective assessment of data that is organised by the SWOT format into a logical order.

This model is often used to support negotiation preparation, as it can help to identify potential leverage against the other party.

Elements

SWOT can be employed to compare the position of both parties in terms of environment and resource capabilities. Figure 1.6 is divided into the four key SWOT areas. The left-hand column refers to business analysis that might typically be undertaken by using this tool, while the right-hand column shows how the SWOT could be applied in the context of a negotiation.

SWOT	Negotiation example
Strengths: These typically refer to internal resources, for example, highly skilled staff, intellectual property rights and/or brand.	**Strengths:** Buyer – internal stakeholder support, good negotiation skills. Seller – good product knowledge, specialist expertise, low costs of manufacture.
Weaknesses: These are the internal weaknesses of the organisation; for example, high overheads, old technology and/or poor internal processes.	**Weaknesses:** Buyer – many internal processes and layers of hierarchy before deal can be signed off. Seller – product of a lower quality than others in the market.
Opportunities: These are external factors that could influence the organisation; for example, a supplier with an opportunity to introduce cost savings.	**Opportunities:** Buyer – could collaborate with another non-competing organisation, i.e., consortium. Seller – competitively priced in the marketplace.
Threats: These are external risk factors; for example, the threat of competition.	**Threats:** Buyer – a duopoly situation, so few sellers in the marketplace. Seller – cheaper suppliers in the marketplace.

Figure 1.6 Elements of a SWOT

So what?

SWOT analysis is normally used in conjunction with a range of other analytical tools as part of a strategic decision-making process, i.e., category/portfolio management.

When used to support negotiation preparation, it can aid development of targets and tradeables, based on analysis drawn from understanding the position of both parties.

Negotiation application

- Helps highlight an organisation's strengths, which can help to make negotiators feel empowered, but can also highlight possible weaknesses and thus risks that need to be explored in a negotiation.
- Helps to determine what opportunities may be available, which could help to create flexibility within the negotiation process.

- Helps to highlight potential threats from the external environment early on, so as to avoid or reduce their effect.
- By looking at both parties' organisations through the SWOT analysis, relative strengths/weaknesses can be determined and planned for accordingly.

Limitations

SWOT is purely a 'snapshot' in time of the status quo. It does not provide direction or next steps. Some critics have argued that SWOT is not really an analytical tool and that it is purely a framework to structure facts and data concerning the current situation.

It should also be noted that there is overlap between SWOT and the well-known PESTLE, (political, economic, sociocultural, technological, legislative and ecological – aka STEEPLE, sociocultural, technological, economic, ecological, political, legislative and ethical) framework, albeit SWOT considers both internal and external factors, while PESTLE only considers external influences.

Further reading

You can read more about SWOT analysis in:

Johnson, G., Scholes, K. and Whittington, R. (2010). *Exploring Strategy: Text and Cases.* 9th edition. Harlow: Prentice Hall.
Boddy, D. and Paton, S. (2010). *Management: An Introduction.* 5th edition. Harlow: Prentice Hall.

Associated template

The following template can be used to support the development of the SWOT analysis:

- Template 4: Negotiation SWOT

PHASE 2

Relationship building

Overview

This is the phase where both parties get to know each other across the negotiating table. Upon initially meeting, discussion will be primarily small talk designed to break the ice, with questions regarding travel, weather, accommodation and how business is doing. Simultaneously, each party will be making an assessment of the other, predominately through the reading of body language.

Once the preliminaries are over with, the conversation should then move to the real issues at hand; speed and flow will be dictated by structure of the agenda.

This section focuses on the key behavioural aspects that are associated with this stage of the negotiation process:

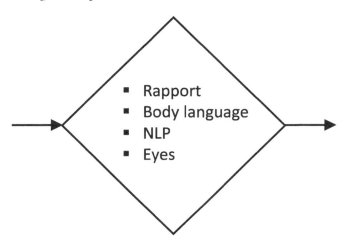

Figure 2.0   Phase 2: Relationship building

5
BUILDING RAPPORT

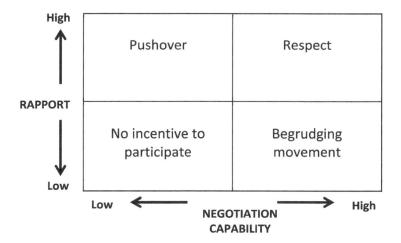

Figure 2.1 The Rapport Matrix

Source: Adapted from Reynolds (2003).

Overview

The Rapport Matrix (Figure 2.1) serves to highlight the importance of combining hard and soft skills when managing stakeholders and conducting negotiations. It considers the need to develop rapport with the other party and consequently establish a relationship within which influencing can be effectively conducted.

Elements

The matrix is based on the skill-base of an individual to create rapport and negotiate respectively. The four quadrants are described as follows:

Pushover – An individual with effective rapport building skills and yet under-developed negotiation capabilities is most likely to be an ineffective negotiator – in essence, a nice person but also a 'pushover' in terms of achieving outcomes.

Respect – The combination of negotiation effectiveness and the ability to develop rapport with others earns respect. This enables collaborative and/or strategic negotiations to be executed more effectively.

No incentive to participate – Inability to create rapport, combined with low negotiation capabilities, can create significant engagement issues for someone wanting to negotiate. They lack the skills required to develop relationships and also to influence others – and therefore give the impression of not participating in the key issues in need of negotiation.

Begrudging movement – This is the classic 'bear-trap' where negotiators focus so intently on their negotiation prowess that they overlook the need to develop rapport and relationships with others. A deal may be able to be brokered and forced through, but resentment and/or adversarialism could accompany the negotiation and have an adverse effect later in the deal.

So what?

The Rapport Matrix provides an excellent illustration of the importance of soft skills within the context of negotiation. It highlights the need for rapport as an important precursor to relationship building and ultimately to the achievement of an effective and successful negotiated outcome.

Negotiation application

- Supports negotiations.
- Useful for developing leadership, influencing and negotiation skills.
- Helps support supplier relationship management activities, where high levels of influencing and persuasion are required.

Limitations

The model is a good *aide memoire* to help remind purchasers the importance of rapport and relationships when negotiating. However, in itself, the model does not tell individuals how they should develop rapport or what skills are required to achieve this. To understand these dimensions of the model, further study of Reynolds' work is required.

Further reading

You can read more about the Rapport Matrix and the development of rapport in:

Reynolds, A. (2003). *Emotional Intelligence and Negotiation*. Hampshire: Tommo Press.

Associated template

The following template can be used when accessing rapport:

• Template 5: Building Rapport.

6
BODY LANGUAGE

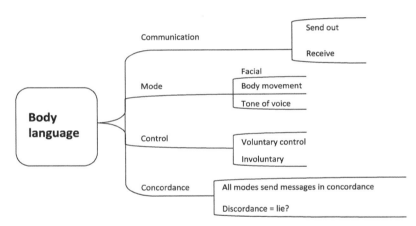

Figure 2.2   Body language

Overview

Body language refers to various forms of non-verbal communication. These behaviours can include body posture, gestures, facial expressions and eye movements. It is thought to be a predominately subconscious behaviour and therefore may provide clues to the attitude or state of mind of an individual.

Albert Mehrabian (1972), a professor well-known for his research on communication, found that there are three basic elements in any face-to-face encounter:

- **Words** – Accounts for 7% of the communication.
- **Tone of voice** – Accounts for 38% of the communication.
- **Non-verbal behaviour** – Accounts for 55% of the communication.

This research has become synonymous with the area of body language and is widely known as the 7%–38%–55% rule or sometimes the '3Vs' for Verbal, Vocal and Visual.

Elements

The study of physical expressions is known as kinesics. The interpretation of body language should not be based on a single sign/gesture. Those observing should look at clusters of information, listen to any verbal cues that link to the sign/gesture and review in the given context. Figure 2.3 shows the most frequently commented-upon body language signals:

Body language	Action	General meaning(s)	Countermeaning
Eyes	Direct eye contact	Honesty, interest, attentiveness.	Trained liars copy this action.
	Widening eyes	Interest, appeal. If paired with raised eyebrows may be a sign of surprise/shock.	Trying to stay awake.
	Rubbing eyes	Usually signifies disbelief, if paired with long blinks then it could mean tiredness or boredom.	An irritant in the eye region may necessitate rubbing.
	Closing eyes momentarily (similar to a lengthy blink)	Thinking of an appropriate response.	Sleepiness.
	Pupils dilated	Attracted to something, excited.	Grows in response to lack of light.
	Blinking (normal blink rate is 6-8 times a minute)	Excitement, pressure. If the blink rate is infrequent it can signify boredom or possibly deep concentration – need to assess the situation carefully.	An irritant in the eye region that may need removing.
Hands	Steepled fingers	Often thought to signify power and confidence.	Popular body language sign copied by those wishing to exhibit powerful and confident behaviour.
	Rubbing hands	Sign of stress. The more frequent the hand rubbing the greater the pressure in the situation. A common comforter or aka a 'pacifier'.	Feeling cold, rubbing hands to gain warmth.
	Chin rubbing	Suggests a judgement is being made.	Recent research has shown that males tend to do this more than females and could be linked to the soothing action of shaving – hence a pacifier.
	Playing with hair	Can reveal an excess of nervous energy, or depending on context a flirtatious gesture. This is also a common comforter.	Common habit regardless of context.
	Stroking of the nose	Linked to lying and referred to as the 'Pinocchio' movement.	May have a genuine itch.

Figure 2.3   Body language signals

Legs and feet	Uncrossed legs while sitting	Interested and open to the conversation.	Should be noted that men generally tend to have a more open leg position than women. Comfort-driven body posture.
	Crossed legs while sitting	Cautious, disinterested, uncertain.	Comfort-driven body posture.
	Ankle lock	Considered to be a negative signal that could mean defensiveness.	Comfort-driven body posture.
	Continuously moving foot whilst legs crossed	Bored, nervous, impatient.	Can sometimes signify rapid thinking.
Arms	Crossed arms	Simulating a protection barrier, often associated with disagreement, disengagement.	Could mean coldness and therefore arms crossed to provide warmth or individuals may fold arms simply for comfort.
	Gripping own upper arms	Associated with insecurity, and therefore an attempt to reassure oneself.	Could mean coldness and therefore arms crossed in hugging position in order to provide warmth.
	Arms behind body with hands clasped	A sign of authority or confidence.	Cultural or sociological influences.

Figure 2.3 Continued

So what?

Much of our body language is emitted unconsciously and therefore the detection of subtle signs and signals can help with the assessment of how others might be thinking and processing information. Even in integrative negotiations, both parties will want to conceal some information concerning their actual negotiation position, therefore the ability to spot 'tells' or subliminal messages through non-verbal communication can help the negotiator make their next move.

Negotiation application

- Enhances the face to face negotiation process.
- Aids communication between the parties.
- Can provide a competitive edge in a negotiation.
- Can support rapport building and mirroring.

Limitations

Body language is a popular subject among negotiation and 'pop psychology' authors. There are many books on the subject; however, much is written from a deductive rather than empirical research perspective. There are some good research papers in existence but these can be difficult to interpret due to the statistical analysis content, and so theories are watered down for the masses. This has meant too much generalisation and oversimplification of the subject.

Students of body language should also be mindful that signs and gestures need to be evaluated in the given context, taking into consideration other factors such as tone of voice and linking actual words to actions.

Finally, it should be noted that the original intent of 'Mehrabian's formula' was to establish the effect of incongruence between words and expressions, i.e., people tended to believe facial expressions more than accompanying tone of voice or words. This is a classic example of how the initial work has been over simplified in order to appeal to a wider audience and no longer bears any resemblance to the original findings.

Further reading

You can read more about the science behind interpreting body language in:

Borg, J. (2013). *Body Language: How to Know What's REALLY Being Said.* 3rd edition. Harlow: Pearson.

Associated template

The following template can be used when looking at body language:

- Template 6: Body Language Observation Sheet.

7

NEURO-LINGUISTIC PROGRAMMING (NLP)

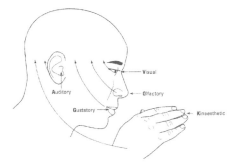

Figure 2.4 NLP

Source: Adapted from Ready and Burton (2015)

Overview

The co-founders of Neuro-Linguistic Programming (NLP), Richard Bandler and John Grinder (1981), believed a connection existed between the neurological processes ('neuro'), language ('linguistic') and behavioural patterns that have been learned through experience ('programming'). Their research into the subject evolved through the 1970s and was being marketed as an essential business communication tool by the end of that decade.

One of the core themes of NLP revolves around 'representational systems' sometimes referred to as 'body language types'. This is predicated on the theory that the way we mentally process information will manifest itself in our body language. The suggestion is that by observing an individual in terms of their speech patterns, gestures, tone of voice, posture and breathing, a particular representational system/body language type can be attributed.

Elements

It is believed that there are five body language types: Visual, Auditory, Kinaesthetic, Olfactory and Gustatory. However, the last two are so rarely identified that NLP practitioners tend to focus their attention on the first three. An explanation of the characteristics thought to exemplar these is as follows:

Visual

A person with a visual preference will tend to process information in terms of viewing/looking at pictures/imagery. Therefore, their language is likely to replicate this with phrases such as:

- **Show** me how it **looks**.
- **Draw** me picture of what that might **look** like.
- It brings **clarity** and **focus**.

Visual types sit forward in meetings, breathing is high in the chest and rate of speech is quite fast. Their hand gestures are likely to be fairly graphic, almost as if they are drawing a picture while talking simultaneously.

Auditory

A person with an auditory preference will tend to process information in terms of sounds. Therefore, their language might appear as:

- This **sounds** good to me.
- That **rings** a **bell** with me.
- We're all **singing** off the same **hymn sheet**.

Auditory types prefer to sit centred rather than forward, breathing is lower in the chest and rate of speech is slower. Their hand gestures on the whole are less graphic, and placed more around the stomach area.

Kinaesthetic

A person with a kinaesthetic preference will tend to process information in terms of feelings/body awareness. Therefore, their language might come across as:

- Something **feels odd**, but I can't put my **finger** on it.
- **I feel** happy about that and can move **forward**.
- I can't get to **grips** with the concept.

Kinaesthetic types feel comfortable sitting back in their chairs. This consequently affects their breathing so that it becomes much slower, and there are very few accompanying hand gestures.

So what?

NLP can provide negotiators with a framework for understanding body language which can enhance communication and dialogue during the negotiation process. Being able to assess and mirror the other party's preferred body language type can apparently deepen rapport and ultimately lessen defensive behaviour.

Many organisations have developed negotiation programmes that include NLP, as it is seen as an enhancement to the 'hard skills' element, and can develop interpersonal sensitivity skills within individuals.

Negotiation application

- Provides a framework for understanding body language.
- Builds rapport quickly rather than waiting for it to occur naturally.
- Can identify own 'body language type' and flex accordingly in order to maximise communication effectiveness.

Limitations

The subject of NLP is extensive, and while much literature exists in the fields of psychotherapy and hypnotherapy, little has been written about NLP and its use within negotiation.

It is a subject that has been largely ignored by conventional social science due to a lack of empirical evidence to substantiate its effectiveness. Indeed, even one of the co-founders, Richard Bandler, has commented that only sometimes do bodily gestures correspond to representation systems.

Further reading

You can read more about the subject of NLP and its core themes in:

Bandler, R. and Grinder, J. (1981). *Frogs into Princes: Neuro Linguistic Programming*. 1st edition. USA: Real People Press.
Ready, R. and Burton, K. (2015). *Neuro-Linguistic Programming for Dummies*. 3rd edition. West Sussex: John Wiley & Sons Ltd.

Associated template

The following test can be used to identify NLP type:

- Template 7: NLP Self-Assessment Test.

8
EYE ACCESSING

Figure 2.5 Eye accessing

Overview

NLP has a number of core themes, one of which is known as 'eye accessing'. Bandler and Grinder (1981) believed they had identified a relationship between the language people use in general conversation and their eye movements. From this they developed a model that depicts the common linkages observed, and suggested that understanding the various eye patterns can help with deciphering how a person is processing information – in other words, a form of mind reading.

Elements

The underpinning research is based on participants in the western hemisphere, the majority of whom are right-handed. Therefore NLP theory states that the patterns relate to the 'common western layout'.

Figure 2.6 outlines the eye accessing cues and should be read as if looking at someone else's face. The type of language that might trigger such movement is also provided through the use of an example question:

Eye accessing cue	Movement	Meaning/language
Visual creation	To the top left	Developing new images Question: Can you imagine how this product might work for you?
Auditory creation	To the side left	Hearing new or different sounds Question: How do you think your boss might respond to this?
Kinaesthetic (feelings)	To the bottom left	Thinking about feelings and emotions Question: Tell me how you feel about this deal?
Visual remembered	To the top right	Seeing old images Question: When was the last time we got together in this room to negotiate?
Auditory remembered	To the side right	Remembering sounds heard before Question: Remind me what I said about this product opportunity last time we met?
Internal dialogue	To the bottom right	Talking to oneself Question: I wonder when they are going to ask me about a discount structure.

Figure 2.6   Elements of eye accessing

So what?

Knowing the eye accessing cues can help to improve body language interpretation during a negotiation. This can ultimately assist with the effective deployment of persuasion methods and tactics. It is also thought that individuals can be influenced to think in a specific way by asking them to visually create the relevant concepts in their mind, and are then helped to develop their thinking via conversation control techniques (see also subliminal linguistics).

Negotiation application

- Provides a framework for understanding eye movements.
- Enhances interpretation of body language.
- Can be useful in discussions to assess how an individual is responding to your ideas.

Limitations

Much of the research into this subject is based on those from the western hemisphere, therefore using this across an international community or a group of left-handers may result in mixed messages! It is also important to remember that the model is only a reflection of what might be happening and some of the patterns can be so slight that misinterpretation can occur.

Further reading

You can read more about the subject of NLP and its core themes in:

Bandler, R. and Grinder, J. (1981). *Frogs into Princes: Neuro Linguistic Programming.* 1st edition. USA: Real People Press.
Ready, R. and Burton, K. (2015). *Neuro-Linguistic Programming for Dummies.* 3rd edition. West Sussex: John Wiley & Sons Ltd.

Associated template

The following template can be used when reviewing eye accessing:

• Template 8: Eye Accessing Observation Sheet.

PHASE 3

Information gathering

Overview

Much preparation surrounding negotiation goals, targets and the BATNA will have taken place prior to the negotiation itself. During Phase 3, assumptions concerning these can be tested to see how realistic they might be.

Gathering information to test such assumptions through the clever use of questioning is vital to the success of this phase.

This section looks at how the negotiator can collect the appropriate data so that it may be used effectively at the next stage of the negotiation process.

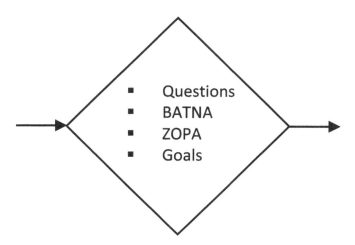

Figure 3.0   Phase 3: Information gathering

9

QUESTIONING TECHNIQUES

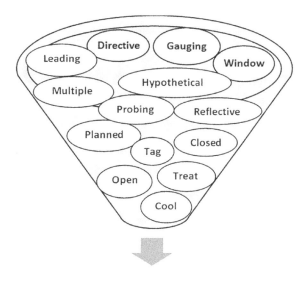

Questioning Techniques?

Figure 3.1 Questioning techniques

Overview

Questions are a key part of the negotiation process. By using the right question, delivered in the correct context the negotiator can prompt a revealing response from the other party. Studies carried out in the late 1970s by Neil Rackham (1996), the founder of the SPIN® questioning methodology, found that average negotiators ask around half as many questions as skilled negotiators.

Many writers have attempted to categorise the range and types of questions that may be used during a negotiation, and while there are some generally well-known ones, there is no definitive list.

Elements

Type of question	Designed to	Example	Advantage/ disadvantage
Open	Invite opinion and alternative perspective from the respondent.	Can you tell me more about your proposal?	☺ Disclosure of information. ☹ Verbose response.
Leading	Lead the respondent to the answer.	That would appear to be the correct option?	☺ Closing down the negotiation. ☹ Can anger the respondent.
Cool	Look as if there is little emotional content attached to the question.	How much more will we be charged?	☺ Poker face. ☹ Negates use of emotion as a persuasion method.
Planned	Be a part of an overall strategy.	Once we've completed round 1 of the negotiations, will you be happier to proceed to contract?	☺ Logical approach . ☹ May be seen as 'too planned' and hurrying.
Treat	Flatter the respondent.	Can you tell me how you managed to make your proposal look so professional?	☺ Use of emotion in order to persuade. ☹ May be viewed as sycophantic.
Window	Provide an insight into the respondent's perspective. Sometimes called the 'open window'.	Can you tell me more about your decision-making process and how you developed it?	☺ Understanding where the respondent is coming from. ☹ Nosey.
Directive	Be direct and to the point.	How much will that price amount to over a period of a year?	☺ No messing around. ☹ Respondent may not be able to cope with approach.
Gauging	Gain the other's perspective.	What are your thoughts so far on the subject?	☺ Rapport building. ☹ Time wasting.
Tag	Elicit consensus while appearing like a question.	I believe we've agreed on that point already, isn't that right?	☺ Appears non-threatening. ☹ May be viewed as manipulative.
Multiple	Gain maximum information by using more than one question.	By what month and by what means do you expect us to improve the situation?	☺ Efficient use of time. ☹ May come across as confusing.
Reflective	Invite reflection upon an issue during the process.	You look a little concerned about the potential outcome?	☺ An opportunity to gain understanding ☹ Time-consuming.
Hypothetical	Provide a scenario in order to clarify/progress a discussion.	What if we decreased the price by a further 2%?	☺ Can test assumptions ☹ Scenario needs to be realistic otherwise not credible.
Closed	Prompt a specific answer such as 'yes' or 'no'.	Can you get a proposal to me by the end of the day?	☺ Effective use of time. ☹ May close down a negotiation.
Probing	Elicit further details/explore situation and/or position.	Can you clarify how you expect us to compete on price?	☺ May create opportunities. ☹ Could go down a metaphorical 'rabbit hole'.

Figure 3.2   Elements of questioning techniques

So what?

A plethora of negotiation authors have cited the use of questioning as a critical success factor when it comes to agreeing an optimal outcome, and have developed complex questioning systems accordingly.

However, the general consensus is that in reality the two most frequently posed questions tend to be simply of the open and closed variety.

Negotiation application

- Important part of the negotiation planning process.
- Can help to create rapport in the negotiation.
- Tests assumptions.
- Enables the communication flow between the parties.
- A way of eliciting agreement.

Limitations

It should be noted that there is a paucity of research in relation to this subject, in part due to the difficulty of capturing live negotiations. Empirical evidence based on such data is available to support Rackham's SPIN® questioning methodology; however, this is regarded as primarily a consultative rather than a negotiation questioning approach.

Further reading

You can read more about questioning techniques in:

Rackham, N. (1996). *The SPIN Selling Fieldbook: Practical Tools, Methods, Exercises and Resources.* New York: McGraw-Hill Professional.
Nierenberg, G.I. (1987). *The Fundamentals of Negotiating.* Reprint edition. New York: Hawthorn Books.

Associated template

The following template can be used to assist questioning during the negotiation:

- Template 9: Questioning Techniques.

10

BATNA

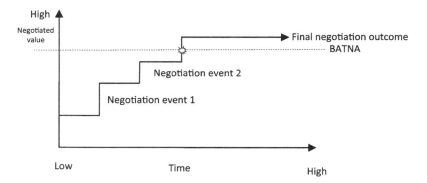

Figure 3.3 BATNA

Overview

BATNA is an acronym for Best Alternative To a Negotiated Agreement and was first coined by negotiation researchers Roger Fisher and William Ury (1997) who worked on the Harvard Negotiation Project.

The BATNA is akin to the negotiator's fall-back position. However, whereas the term fall-back infers that the agreement reached may be sub-optimal, the BATNA is viewed as an alternative to reaching a mutually acceptable settlement. The basic premise is that a negotiator should not accept a worse resolution than their BATNA.

Similarly the BATNA should not be confused with the walk-away point, which suggests that there is no alternative option.

Elements

Know your BATNA	It is important to know the point at which you can say no to an unfavourable proposal. A strong BATNA may determine a more advantageous outcome, whereas a weak BATNA could put you in a less favourable position.
Improving your BATNA	You may wish to improve your BATNA by creating more alternatives, thus increasing your power in the negotiation.
Disclose your BATNA	At some stage during the negotiation process it may be beneficial to disclose your BATNA, i.e., naming alternative sources of supply.
Consider the other side's BATNA	Knowledge of the other side's BATNA is another source of negotiation strength. Being able to ascertain their position in comparison to your own could provide you with a considerable advantage, especially if you can find a way of weakening their alternative.
BATNA-less	*'The BATNA-less party is a deal taker, not a deal maker.'* Theorists suggest that if you find yourself in this position you should immediately create a BATNA.

Figure 3.4   Elements of BATNA

So what?

Being BATNA-less means that you are more likely to accept a deal rather than negotiate it. Therefore, determining a strong yet flexible BATNA is the key to a successful outcome. However, how do you know if you have set the BATNA correctly? Some academics suggest the following process:

1. Brainstorm a range of alternative options in the event that the negotiation fails to reach an agreement.
2. Choose the most promising and expand them into practical and attainable goals.
3. Assess the strength of the options, i.e., strong/weak, as this will help you to decide whether they should be revealed to the other side
4. Rank the options in order to determine your 'prime BATNA'.

The willingness of a negotiator to break off a negotiation (invoking the BATNA) will allow them to adopt a firmer stance during the bidding phase of the negotiation process – in essence delivering the threat of walking away.

Negotiation application

- Planning the negotiation strategy (integrative/distributive).
- Preparing opening statements.
- Establishing targets and ranges.
- Post-negotiation evaluation.

Limitations

Developed in the early 1980s, the BATNA theory appears to split academics. Many argue that it is more suited to industrial relations negotiations, while others promote it as a negotiation fundamental. A concept that has been gathering momentum is that of EATNA – Estimated Alternative To a Negotiated Agreement. This allows for the many instances where negotiators believe they have a powerful alternative when in actual fact they do not.

Further reading

You can read more about BATNA in:

Fisher, R., Ury, W. and Patton, B. (1982). *Getting to Yes: Negotiating an Agreement Without Giving In*. 1st edition. London: Hutchinson Paperback.

Associated template

The following template can be used to support the development of the BATNA:

- Template 10: BATNA.

11
ZOPA

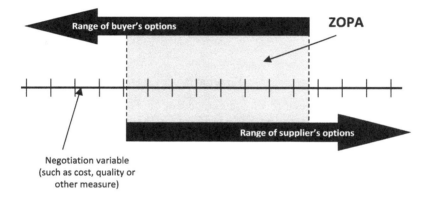

ZOPA

Range of buyer's options

Range of supplier's options

Negotiation variable
(such as cost, quality or
other measure)

Figure 3.5 ZOPA

Source: Adapted from Harvard Business School

Overview

Initially this model was used as a tool for dispute resolution and often associated with the BATNA negotiation approach (Best Alternative To a Negotiated Agreement – Fisher et al., 1982). The Zone of Possible Agreement (ZOPA) describes the area where agreement may be met between two parties.

ZOPA is about setting targets of a negotiation and minimum 'fall-back' positions. The limits of ZOPA represent each party's fall-back position, below which either party would 'walk away'. Therefore it is suggested that once both sides have moved into their respective zones (i.e., beyond the fall-back), then it is more probable that consensus will be reached.

Elements

To initiate this process an opening offer needs to be made by one of the parties. This in turn will be evaluated by the receiving party who will take a decision whether to respond or not, and if so in which zone. This will continue until the ZOPA is reached and an acceptable agreement is formulated within the zone. The range of options within the ZOPA is as follows:

Reasonable Zone – Considered as the precursor to the ZOPA. It is thought that an opening offer in this region is reasonable enough to be able to move towards a mutually acceptable agreement.

Credible Zone – An opening offer here may be perceived as slightly unreasonable and therefore may or may not set a parameter for negotiation.

Extreme Zone – An offer opened in this zone will not usually set the parameter for negotiation; however, those offers that are deemed 'extreme but credible' may trigger movement.

Insult Zone – Considered so unreasonable that it not only fails to set the parameter for negotiation, but it may also cause the other party to refuse to continue discussions.

So what?

The ZOPA demonstrates the various positions that can be taken when attempting to reach agreement. This can provide a platform for offer and concession in order to obtain a mutually acceptable resolution.

When establishing a fall-back position it is important to remember to develop a package of variables in order to create a bargaining mix with which to negotiate. It is also necessary to identify those variables that are 'throwaways' and those that are 'trade-offs', so that concessions can be elicited from the other party who may place more value on them.

Negotiation application

- Useful planning tool to create a negotiation strategy.
- Supports commercial negotiations and contractual disputes.

Limitations

This model does not take into account the relative strengths, power or interests of the parties, all of which can have an effect upon the process. It also ignores the impact of new information gleaned during the course of an agreement, which can either enhance or limit a party's ability to respond.

The model is predicated on the principal persuasion tools of bargaining and compromise – the weakest forms of negotiation.

Finally, critics have suggested that this model fails to allow for creativity (i.e., through the joint exploration of issues), because each party's fall-back position is already predetermined.

Further reading

You can read more about ZOPA in:

Lax, D.A. and Sebenius, J.K. (1986). *The Manager as Negotiator: Bargaining for Cooperation and Competitive Gain.* New York: The Free Press.
Lewicki, R.J., Barry, B. and Saunders, D.M. (2010). *Negotiation.* 6th edition. New York: McGraw-Hill.

Associated template

The following template can be used to support the development of the ZOPA:

* Template 11: ZOPA.

12

NEGOTIATION GOALS
AND TARGETS

Figure 3.6   Negotiation goals and targets

Overview

Goal setting theory was developed by Edwin A Locke in the 1960s (Locke and Latham 1984). His work proved there was a positive relationship between clearly identified goals and performance. Subsequent research has shown that challenging goals can lead to higher performance.

The acronym SMART, which stands for specific, measurable, achievable, realistic and time-bound, is often used when establishing goals. Goals that are agreed rather than imposed are thought more likely to yield success.

Elements

Goals are often referred to as targets in negotiation and one of the most popular ways of classifying them is shown in Figure 3.7.

Target	Description	Example
Ideal	A 'stretch' goal is set significantly higher than the fall-back position – the perfect outcome.	25% discount
Optimal	A more realistic goal, but still higher than the fall-back position – best outcome we can expect.	15% discount
Fall-back	An acceptable position if ideal or optimal cannot be reached – worst possible scenario but still able to accept.	10% discount
Walk-away	The point at which agreement cannot be gained and one party 'walks away'.	<10% discount

Figure 3.7   Elements of negotiation targets

Another popular method of setting targets is to use the acronym MIL, originated by Dr Gavin Kennedy (1998), formerly Emeritus Professor at Heriot-Watt University. He suggested the following as framework:

- **M**ust achieve – objectives and goals that must be achieved in order to come to agreement.
- **I**ntend to achieve – represents an optimal target of achievement.
- **L**ike to achieve – 'extras', which are nice to have rather than necessarily needed.

So what?

The development of a range of targets can help to motivate individuals during the negotiation process. Target setting is considered one of the main constituents of negotiation planning and will predicate where you position your opening marker.

Setting goals and targets can also aid in personal development as they act as a measure of quantifiable achievement. It can be a useful self-development activity to check the accuracy and the appropriateness of the goals and targets initially set once the negotiation has been completed.

Negotiation application

- Can motivate the negotiator to improve their performance.
- Helps the individual/team to set the tone for the negotiation, i.e., hard or soft approach.
- Can be used as a basis for measurement.
- Provides a focus for the team/individual.

Limitations

In addition to being SMART, there are a number of other caveats that should be considered when setting goals and targets, such as subjectivity, individual capability and buy-in to the process. It should be noted that goals and targets that are 'too stretching' can result in either an impasse or win-lose situation where one party may feel aggrieved with the final outcome.

BATNA can sometimes be confused with walk-away. BATNA suggests there is an alternative position, whereas walk-away is the point of no agreement whether an alternative exists or not. The presence of a meaningful BATNA will therefore strengthen the walk-away position and therefore the overall negotiation.

Further reading

You can read more about setting negotiation targets in:

Lewicki, R.J., Barry, B. and Saunders, D.M. (2010). *Negotiation*. 6th edition. New York: McGraw-Hill.
Kennedy, G. (2003). *Perfect Negotiation*. 2nd edition. London: Random House Business Books.

Associated template

The following template can be used to support the development of negotiation goals and targets:

- Template 12: Negotiation Goals and Targets

PHASE 4

Information using

Overview

Once assumptions have been tested and it is evident that there is an appetite to negotiate between the parties, the information collated during the previous phase can be used to develop a positioning plan. For example, this could entail prioritising tradeables and formulating a suitable opening offer.

At this stage it is also important for the negotiator to remember what power they may have in their armoury, both from an organisational and a personal perspective. However, the strength of their pursuant debate may depend somewhat upon their personality.

This section reviews the key elements to take into consideration before making the first move:

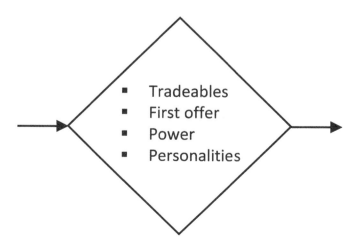

- Tradeables
- First offer
- Power
- Personalities

Figure 4.0   Phase 4: Information using

13

TRADEABLES AND STRAW ISSUES

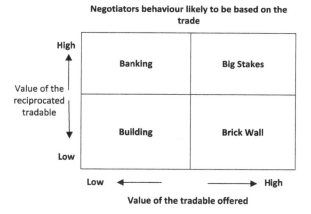

Figure 4.1 The tradeables evaluation model

Overview

Dr Chester L. Karrass (1993), an author on negotiation, states that 'issues are created – some are real and some are made of straw', hence the term 'straw issue'. These are areas of potential contention that can be introduced into the negotiation to either confuse, mask a real problem or trade in order to gain a more valuable concession from the other party. The concept of the straw issue is frequently linked to the word 'tradeable', although they should not be interpreted as meaning the same.

Tradeables on the other hand are negotiation variables that have been identified as potential bargaining chips to be offered to the other party so that something of more value may be achieved in return. Based on the psychology of giving, the tradeable is said to foster feelings of gratitude and positivity in the receiving party and therefore similar concession behaviour is expected to occur.

Elements

The tradeables evaluation model assesses the potential response of a negotiator based on their perceived value of a reciprocated concession:

- **Banking** – Negotiator offers something of low value and is given a high value concession in return. The negotiator banks the proceeds and continues to bargain in the same manner.
- **Big Stakes** – Negotiator offers a tradeable of high value and is given high value in return. This is a high stakes bargaining scenario and the negotiator may wish to continue similar behaviour or attempt to move to the Banking quadrant.
- **Brick Wall** – Negotiator offers a tradeable of high value and is given a low value concession by the other party in return. The negotiator could feel like they have 'hit a brick wall' and may need to rethink their bargaining strategy.
- **Building** – Negotiator offers something of low value and is given a low value concession in return. The negotiator may continue to bargain in the same manner in the hope of eventually moving into the Banking quadrant or may need to rethink their strategy and offer high value concessions in order to increase the pace of the bargaining process.

Figure 4.2 shows some of the most common tradeables observed during the negotiation process, deployed to improve the overall value of the deal:

Tradeable	Example
Volume	'If you could give me more volume I could give you more discount.'
Extension of warranty	'I can extend your computer warranty from one to two years if you could improve my payment terms.'
Introductions/ reference site	'I could add additional resource free of charge to service your regional contract if you could introduce us to other areas within your business.'
Payment terms	'I can include an "out of hours" service in the overall price if you could improve your payment terms from 30 to 14 days.'
Delivery	'If you could deliver free of charge, we could look at renewing the contract.'
Quality	'If quality targets are exceeded, we can look at an incentivisation plan.'

Figure 4.2 Tradeable elements

Tradeable	Example
Use of trade marks	'You can use our trademark, if we could use your specialist in this area free of charge for two days to help us with a project.'
Retention of monies	'We will reduce the retention period, if you can deliver early.'
Service levels/response times	'If you could improve your response times, we could increase the scope of the contract.'
Exclusivity	'You will be our exclusive supplier if we can agree an improved price.'
Insurance parameters	'Can we agree to reduce the liquidated damages liability, in return for an improved delivery date.'
Basis for contract terms	'We will agree to your contract terms, if you can agree that we will get the contract signed by the end of the month.'
Intellectual property rights	'Let's split the proceeds on the newly developed product.'

Figure 4.2 Continued

So what?

Both straw issues and tradeables can provide room for the negotiator to manoeuvre and improve competitive advantage. Creating a wide range of tradeables can increase bargaining flexibility and affords options in the event of deadlock.

It is also thought that the process of bargaining tradeables to achieve a desired outcome can help to alleviate the effects of 'buyer's remorse' – a marketing term used to describe how individuals become increasingly unsatisfied with their purchase the higher the price paid. This unease can be offset if the purchaser believes that there are additional benefits/concessions associated with the initial shopping tag.

Negotiation application

- Can help to create negotiation leverage.
- Bargaining tradeables can appear like a win–win strategy.
- Can create flexibility and new opportunities in the negotiation.
- Some cultures prefer to negotiate based on the psychology of giving.

Limitations

Giving in order to receive is accepted doctrine in negotiation. However, it should be noted that relying solely on bargaining could weaken one's ability to gain the most competitive advantage, as more powerful methods such as threat are being ignored (see Phase 5, Section 17 Persuasion Methods).

Evaluating the value of a concession to the other party and identifying the right time to concede can be very challenging. Successful bargaining will therefore depend upon the negotiator's skill, judgement and intuition in order to ensure that the Banking quadrant is where the majority of the trading activity takes place. This is not an easy task to undertake during the heat of the negotiation process.

Further reading

You can read more about the psychology behind tradeables and straw issues in:

Kennedy, G. (2003). *Perfect Negotiation.* 2nd edition. London: Random House Business Books.

Cialdini, R.B. (2007). *Influence: The Psychology of Persuasion.* Revised edition. New York: HarperBusiness.

Chamoun-Nicolas, H. and Hazlett, R.D. (2007). *Negotiate like a Phonenician: Discover Tradeables.* Houston: Key-Negotiations.

Associated template

The following template can be used to prioritise tradeables and straw issues:

• Template 13: Tradeables and Straw Issues

14

FIRST OFFER

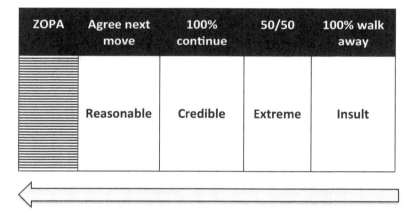

ZOPA	Agree next move	100% continue	50/50	100% walk away
	Reasonable	Credible	Extreme	Insult

Figure 4.3 Responses to the first offer

Overview

The question of whether to make the opening offer in a negotiation plagues buyers and sellers alike. Lacking the complete picture about an opponent's bargaining position can be disconcerting, and psychological analysis shows that most negotiators who make first offers are not aggressive enough.

Because of the inherent ambiguity surrounding the 'first move', the general consensus is to wait for the other party to reveal their hand, aka putting down a marker. However, many sales experts believe that making a sufficiently 'tough' opening stance at the beginning of the negotiation process can bring about a significant competitive advantage.

Elements

There are a multitude of factors to take into account when considering whether to place an opening offer:

- **The psychology of anchoring** – First offers have an anchoring effect, i.e., they have a strong influence on the remainder of the negotiation.
- **Personality** – Confidence/assertiveness/competitiveness can help the negotiator to make the initial move.
- **Preparation** – Facts and data can be a source of expert power for the negotiator.
- **BATNA** – An alternative strategy in the event of non-agreement (see Phase 3, Section 10 BATNA) can underpin a strong opener.
- **Culture** – Some cultures are more at ease with conflict and tension in a commercial discussion, which can provide a natural platform for positioning a tough marker.
- **ZOPA** – The placement of the opening offer along the agreement continuum (see Phase 3, Section 11 ZOPA).

ZOPA	Strength of opening offer	Negotiation impact
Insult	Very tough, unreasonable opening offer.	100% likely that negotiation will not proceed.
Extreme	Very tough, but may be acceptable.	50/50 chance of negotiation proceeding.
Credible	Tough, but acceptable.	100% likely that negotiation will proceed.
Reasonable	Acceptable	100% likely that negotiation will proceed and reach conclusion.

Figure 4.4   Elements of responses

Note: The 'extreme but credible marker' theory is based on the information contained in Figure 4.4 and is thought to be the best starting point, i.e., midway between the extreme and credible.

So what?

Upon entering into a negotiation it is doubtful that all the facts relating to the situation are known to the parties and this could mean hesitance on both sides in proffering a marker in order to commence the process. Each will need to prepare in advance what their strategy will be in these circumstances. At least by planning for this eventuality, an attempt to develop an extreme but credible marker can be made thus ensuring adequate room to manoeuvre during the negotiation.

Many negotiation training courses suggest letting the opposition put forward the first offer. In contrast, the majority of sales-orientated training courses advocate the reverse. One rule of thumb when deciding which option is best is to assess your line of attack, i.e., a distributive approach lends itself to making an opening offer, but when being more accommodative let the other side have the honour.

Negotiation application

- Useful planning tool when developing a negotiation strategy.
- Helps the individual/team to set the tone for the negotiation, i.e., hard or soft approach.
- Can be used as a basis for post-negotiation evaluation.
- Provides a focus for the team/individual.

Limitations

There is inadequate research to support an assertion either way. Pros and cons of each are muted, but it must be remembered that in large part, the personal attributes, experience and skill of the negotiator will also dictate how the negotiation will be initiated.

It is certainly more difficult to quantify the exact point at which maximum advantage will be gained – the extreme but credible marker – making it a high risk strategy to reveal your hand first. Too tough and the risk is the negotiation disintegrates, too soft and the risk is paying too high a price.

Finally, it should be noted that determining what makes a tough opening offer will vary greatly from culture to culture depending upon variables such as preferred persuasion method, conflict style and attitude to ambiguity.

Further reading

You can read more about setting negotiation targets in:

Kennedy, G. (2003). *Perfect Negotiation*. 2nd edition. London: Random House Business Books.
Lax, D.A. and Sebenius, J.K. (1986). *The Manager as Negotiator: Bargaining for Cooperation and Competitive Gain*. New York: The Free Press.
Lewicki, R.J., Barry, B. and Saunders, D.M. (2010). *Essentials of Negotiation*. 6th edition. London: McGraw-Hill.
Galinsky, A. and Musseriler, T. (2010). First offers as anchors: the role of perspective-taking and negotiator focus, *Journal of Personality and Social Psychology*, 81(4), 657–669.

Associated template

The following template can be used to support the development of the first offer:

- Template 14: First Offer.

15

NEGOTIATION POWER

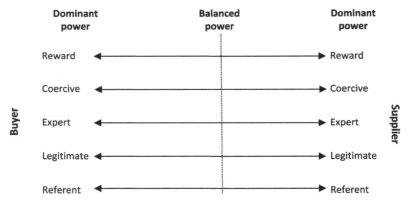

Figure 4.5 The primary powers

Overview

Negotiation and power are closely linked. Social power is the term used to describe the types available to an individual that could be applied to influence others. One of the most credible studies on social power was conducted by psychologists John French and Bertram Raven (1959) in the late 1950s. Their original research looked at the perceived power in a dyadic relationship.

French and Raven initially identified six categories of power; however, over time this has been distilled down to the five 'primary powers' classification, which has proved to be a more popular grouping.

Elements

The five primary powers are commonly regarded as:

- **Reward power** – The ability to provide compensation for compliance.
- **Coercive power** – The ability to punish in the event of non-compliance.
- **Legitimate power** – The ability via authority/position to demand compliance.
- **Expert power** – The ability to command respect via skill and knowledge.
- **Referent power** – The ability to exert power as a result of charisma, charm and personal appeal.

Examples of perceived power in negotiations are shown in Figure 4.6.

Power	Buyer	Supplier
Reward	Award of the contract/additional work.	Discount/additional value/'extras'.
Coercive	Rescind the contract/alternative sources of supply/reduce scope.	Take away resources/stop work.
Legitimate	Ability to agree/not agree the deal.	Ability to agree/not agree the deal.
Expert	Knowledge of the buying process/competitors offers.	Knowledge of the product/market.
Referent	Negotiation/influencing skills and experience.	Negotiation/influencing skills and experience.

Figure 4.6 Examples of the perceived powers

So what?

Research suggests that the most effective leaders use mainly referent and expert power, which is aligned to personality and experience, also sometimes referred to as 'personal power'. Personal power takes advantage of the individual's relationship with others.

Reward, coercive and legitimate power, alternatively known as 'positional power', can be seen as distributive, due to their 'chain and command' nature.

Personality and trait theorists posit that 'extroverts' are more likely to use positional power, while 'introverts' prefer an interpersonal connection and, therefore, lean more heavily on referent power.

Negotiation application

- Identify hidden sources of influence being applied during the process.
- Assess the personal power of the other party and counteract accordingly.
- Recognise own sources of power.
- Helps to provide additional intangible leverage.

Limitations

Social power is a good reminder to individuals of their own personal power in a negotiation; however, it is important to remember the other sources that may exist between the parties such as size, capacity, growth potential and so on.

Over use of power such as market position and size can seriously harm a buyer–supplier relationship, placing one party in a dominant position and the other potentially feeling manipulated, and as such does not engender the concept of partnership.

Finally it is worth noting that the French and Raven model is based on perception (i.e., perceived power) and that therefore kidology has a part to play in exaggerating and/or neutralising one's position in a negotiation.

Further reading

You can read more about negotiation power in:

Kennedy, G. (2003). *Perfect Negotiation*. 2nd edition. London: Random House Business Books.

Lewicki, R.J., Barry, B. and Saunders, D.M. (2010). *Essentials of Negotiation*. 6th edition. London: McGraw-Hill.

Associated template

The following template can be used to assess negotiation power:

- Template 15: Negotiation Power.

16
PERSONALITIES

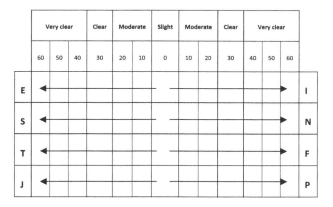

	Very clear			Clear	Moderate	Slight	Moderate	Clear	Very clear		
	60	50	40	30	20	10	0	10	20	30	40	50	60

E ←————————————————————————→ I

S ←————————————————————————→ N

T ←————————————————————————→ F

J ←————————————————————————→ P

Figure 4.7   Myers Briggs personality type indicator

Overview

According to the eminent psychologist Dr Carl Jung (1971), we will frequently revert to our persona in response to workplace demands in order to protect ourselves 'against vulnerability'.

Many organisations employ psychological profiling tools to develop their understanding in this complex field, most of which are founded work done by Jung nearly 100 years ago. The most commonly used is the Myers Briggs Type Indicator® (MBTI), which has more than 50 years of empirical evidence to support it and is regarded as the 'gold standard' across all industries. It has been translated into more than 60 languages and modified to suit a wide range of cultures.

According to research, being able to 'speed read' the other party's personality in a negotiation using a personality assessment instrument such as MBTI can produce better negotiated outcomes.

Elements

The concept of MBTI is based on four main personality strands. It is thought that individuals will have a preference at either end of a spectrum for each of these. This therefore equates to 16 generic personality types in total, i.e., 4 × 4 preferences.

The four main personality strands aka dichotomies are as follows:

- **Extraversion** (E) or **Introversion** (I) – Does the individual prefer to focus on the outer world, i.e., talk to others, or on their own inner world, i.e., think things through by oneself before engaging others?
- **Sensing** (S) or **Intuition** (N) – Does the individual prefer to engage with facts or are they happy to operate in an environment of ambiguity?
- **Thinking** (T) or **Feeling** (F) – When making a decision does the individual prefer to base it on logic and consistency or values, i.e., looking at the people involved and their circumstances?
- **Judging** (J) or **Perceiving** (P) – When managing daily routines/life, does the individual prefer to plan and be organised, or have added adrenalin through leaving everything to the last minute?

Once an individual has decided upon which end of the spectrum they reside, they can identify their personality type which is expressed as a four letter code.

The 16 personality types are shown in Figure 4.8 in what is often referred to as a 'type table'.

ISTJ	ISFJ	INFJ	INTJ
ISTP	ISFP	INFP	INTP
ESTP	ESFP	ENFP	ENTP
ESTJ	ESFJ	ENFJ	ENTJ

Figure 4.8 Type table

It should be noted that no single personality type is better than any other, nor is this an indication of skill and ability. It is about understanding one's preferences only.

So what?

MBTI assessment is commonly used in organisations to assess and develop teams. Understanding the preferences of others in the workplace can support effective working practices and effective communication. In the context of negotiation, it could be used to enhance team dynamics between stakeholders/the negotiation project team, and externally to gauge the possible negotiation style(s) of those from the other party. For example, some personality types have a preference for negotiating on the basis of logic due to their structured approach to decision making coupled with their reliance on data (E and J), whereas others may prefer to negotiate using the tool of emotion that is predicated upon the personality trait of intuitive thinking (N).

Once the basic theory of MBTI is understood, it is fairly easy to 'speed read' another person, which makes it a useful tool to include within the negotiation process.

Negotiation application

- Supports understanding of how others like to work and operate within a team environment.
- Can be used to assess the other party and their preferred negotiation style.
- A useful model to help develop an individual's negotiation skill, through the development of interpersonal sensitivity.
- Helpful to individuals to know their own preferences so that they can accommodate others.

Limitations

Even though the MBTI measurement instrument is regarded as pre-eminent in its field, it still has its detractors. The accuracy of the tool is dependent upon honest self-assessment, and therefore it is argued that individuals can fake their responses and skew their personality result, perhaps to fit in with others or to be the only one, for example.

Whilst a correlation can be made between personality preferences and negotiation styles, it still does not suggest what type(s) make the 'best negotiator', or the skills needed to be a good negotiator. Indeed, at this stage there is still no empirical evidence in existence that can answer such a question, even though some authors state 'warm but tough', assertive, effective listening, etc., this is purely conjecture.

There are also many other personality assessment tools in existence based on Carl Jung's teachings, which could be better suited to organisations/individuals, but most will invariably be self-assessment like the MBTI, which means that the efficacy of results is reliant upon those reporting them.

Further reading

You can read more about personalities in:

Jung, C.G. (1971). *Psychological Types (Collected works of C.G. Jung, Volume 6).* 3rd edition. Princeton, NJ: Princeton University Press. First appeared in German in 1921.
Myers-Briggs, I. (2000). *Introduction to Type.* 6th edition. Revised edition by L.K. Kirby and K.D. Myers. California: CPP Inc.

Associated template

The following template can be used for personality assessment:

- Template 16: Personality and Negotiation Self-Assessment Guide.

PHASE 5

Bidding

Overview

The bidding phase involves each party declaring their opening offer and then making moves towards agreeing a mutually acceptable outcome.

Utilising the five main methods of persuasion will help to drive the bidding process, while various influencing techniques and tactics can be deployed as a quick means to gaining additional concessions.

The more resilient, flexible and adaptable the individual, the more likely it is that they will be able to survive a long and complex negotiation, therefore the emotional intelligence profile of the negotiator should also be considered.

This section focuses on the part of the process where the majority of the negotiation activity takes place.

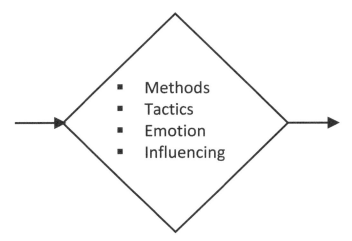

Figure 5.0   Phase 5: Bidding

17

PERSUASION METHODS

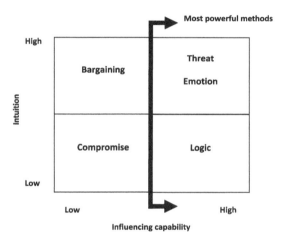

Figure 5.1   Persuasion methods
Source: Adapted from Reynolds (2003).

Overview

The concept of a range of persuasion tools used in negotiation emanated from F.K. Berrien (1944), a professor of psychology in the early 1940s. This idea was later developed by a team of psychologists and resulted in a popular framework listing five persuasion tools that are commonly exhibited across a broad spectrum of negotiations.

These five are known as Compromise, Bargaining, Emotion, Logic and Threat and the initial letters form the acronym C-BELT. The C is often shown slightly apart, as the persuasion method of compromise is considered to be the weakest persuasion tool.

Elements

The five persuasion methods that form the basis of many negotiation programmes are outlined in Figure 5.2.

Persuasion Tool	Description	Advantages	Disadvantages
Compromise	Negotiating using concessions that are based on something of value. Example: 'Let's split the difference' or 'Let's meet in the middle'.	• Easy to use • Least confrontational • Quick • Good tool to use at the end of the negotiation process.	• Concede something of value • Can be perceived as a weak negotiator if used at the outset of the negotiation process.
Bargaining	Negotiating using concessions that are based on 'straw issues', i.e., of little value. Example: 'If you can give me 5% discount then I can reduce payment terms.' The word 'If' is often used in bargaining.	• Easy to use • A 'bargaining flow' can occur quite quickly if the other party also uses it • Viewed as a 'win/win' approach.	• 'Straw issue' will still have a minimal value attached to it • A pattern of concession giving may make it difficult to switch to alternative persuasion tools.
Emotion	Negotiating using emotion to move the other party without providing any concession. Example: 'The offer you have put forward is insulting and I'm disappointed.'	• Negotiating without concession • Fairly non-confrontational.	• Can be difficult to deploy effectively • If overplayed can be seen as 'cheesy'.
Logic	Negotiating using facts and data to substantiate your position. Example: 'The current inflation rate suggests there should be no increase applied to the contract.'	• Negotiating without concession • Difficult to argue/negotiate against.	• Can lose credibility if facts/data/logic incorrect • The negotiation can reach impasse if the other party is also using logic.
Threat	Negotiating using an implied or explicit threat, i.e., consequences applied to non-compliance. Example: 'If you don't lower your rates we'll find another supplier.'	• Negotiating without concession • Powerful tool that can have an immediate effect.	• Confrontational • Can ruin the negotiation dynamics/relationship • Can be perceived as a win-lose approach.

Figure 5.2 Elements of the five persuasion methods

So what?

Having a theoretical framework can help the negotiator to try out the various tools during a negotiation. If one fails to achieve a response then an alternative option can be used. Also, being able to recognise the tools as they are played across the negotiation table can assist with appropriate counteraction.

Research has shown that inexperienced negotiators tend to use compromise as this is the easiest and least confrontational, whereas strong negotiators with a high level of intuition tend to prefer the persuasion methods of threat and emotion.

Understanding the full range of methods available can promote greater flexibility and adaptability during negotiation.

Negotiation application

- Provides a framework for the negotiator.
- Can link choice of persuasion methods to overall negotiation strategy, i.e., integrative or distributive.
- Avoids the 'negotiator's cul-de-sac'.
- Can identify own preferences and develop a more rounded suite of capability.

Limitations

There are a multitude of theorists on negotiation, in particular the Harvard Negotiation Project, which is world renowned for its research on the subject. Some do not subscribe to the Berrien view and prefer to think in terms of bargaining only, of which the remaining four persuasion methods form a part.

Further reading

You can read more about the five main persuasion methods and accompanying underpinning psychology in:

Berrien, F.K. (1944). *Practical Psychology*. New York: Macmillan.
Brown, J.M., Berrien, F.K., Russell, D.L. and Wells, W.D. (1966). *Applied Psychology*. New York: Macmillan.
Kennedy, G. (2003). *Perfect Negotiation*. 2nd edition. London: Random House Business Books.

Associated template

The following template can be used to assess the use of persuasion methods:

- Template 17: Persuasion Methods.

18

NEGOTIATION TACTICS

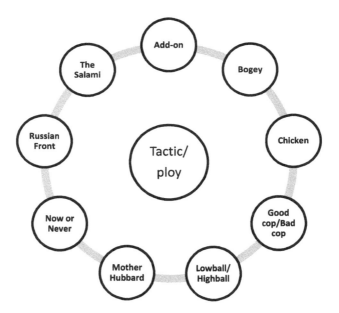

Figure 5.3   Negotiation tactics

Overview

There are a plethora of different tactics used in the negotiation process. Some authors like to split them into either integrative or distributive approaches; however, most are happy to just consider them as short-term tactical solutions to gaining competitive edge.

Tactics are normally employed at the bidding stage of the negotiation process, and are frequently used alongside the persuasion and influencing tools.

Elements

Negotiation tactics should align with the overall negotiation strategy. Some of the most popular tactics are listed in Figure 5.4.

Tactic	Description
Add-on	Tell the other party that the agreed price does not include various extras, all of which have to be paid for separately.
Bogey	Intimate that a trivial issue is very important, with the intention of trading this issue later for a major concession.
Chicken	Make an extravagant demand and bluff that it must be accepted 'or else'.
Good cop/Bad cop	Explains how much you sympathise with the other party's view, but 'unfortunately' you have a much tougher boss who won't allow you much leeway.
Lowball/Highball	Begin the negotiation with a ridiculously low (or high) offer, hoping that the other party will re-evaluate their own opening offer.
Mother Hubbard	Tell the other party that you love doing business with them, but 'the cupboard is bare' – you just have no further leeway on the issues under debate.
Now or Never	Hurry the other party to accept quickly – 'we can't hold this price beyond today'.
Russian Front	Present two alternatives, one of them so awful (the Russian front) that the other party may be forced into accepting the other.
The Salami	Slicing a big issue into a collection of smaller ones and try for movement on each individual piece.

Figure 5.4   Elements of negotiation tactics

So what?

The use of tactics during a negotiation can open up opportunities where perhaps the persuasion and influencing methods have failed. They should be seen as extra armoury within the individual's 'negotiation tool kit', and it is important to use them as the occasion befits. Many may be inappropriate or too obvious, thus care needs to be taken.

Knowing how you might react and counteract these various tactics is also an important factor to consider when planning for the negotiation.

Negotiation application

- Used within the bidding phase to complement persuasion and influencing methods.
- Can create negotiation manoeuvrability.
- May provide quick wins.

Limitations

Tactics are 'quick plays', and regardless of their integrative or distributive nature, the negotiation dynamics have to be conducive to their utilisation, otherwise they may be quickly seen for what they are. Some negotiators dismiss the use of tactics and prefer to focus on their strategic process to deliver desired outcomes, arguing that this will lessen the need for 'nickel and diming' in the short term.

Further reading

You can read more about tactics in:

Lewicki, R.J., Barry, B. and Saunders, D.M. (2010). *Essentials of Negotiation*. 6th edition. London: McGraw-Hill.

Associated template

The following template can be used to assess negotiation tactics:

- Template 18: Negotiation Tactics.

19
EMOTIONAL INTELLIGENCE

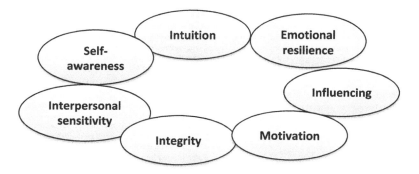

Figure 5.5   Emotional intelligence

Overview

The concept of emotional intelligence (EI) was popularised by Daniel Goleman (1996). He posits that in order to be successful, individuals need both their Intelligence Quotient (IQ) and their Emotional Quotient (EQ) to be higher than average. Similar to IQ, an individual's EQ can be measured.

In 2002, research undertaken at Henley Management College revealed that there were significant links between the EQ of procurement professionals and their ability to negotiate. These findings have been linked to persuasion styles and a framework developed that can highlight individual preferences.

Elements

Elements of emotional intelligence	Link to negotiation
Self-awareness Awareness of own feelings and the ability to recognise and manage those feelings. Also includes a degree of self-belief in the ability to manage emotions, and their subsequent manifestation in a work environment.	Key at initial stages of the negotiation process, when stakeholders and key users need to be brought on board. Also helps the negotiator to manage feelings during the 'bidding' phase.
Emotional resilience Ability to perform consistently in a range of situations under pressure and consequently adapt behaviour. Can balance needs of situation and task with those of individuals. Retains focus in the face of personal challenge and criticism.	Essential that the negotiator maintains a high degree of emotional resilience when facing difficult and uncompromising opposition. The ability to maintain a positive outlook when facing rejection, and to keep going in the face of potential defeat.
Motivation Drive and energy to achieve clear results, make an impact and balance short- and long-term goals with an ability to pursue demanding goals in the face of rejection or questioning.	High motivation is linked to achieving stretching negotiation targets. The more determined and focused the negotiator, the bigger the potential prize.
Interpersonal sensitivity Ability to be aware of, and take account of, the needs and perceptions of others in arriving at the decisions and proposing solutions to problems and challenges. The ability to build from this awareness and achieve the commitment of others to decisions and action ideas. Actively listening to, and reflecting on, the reactions and inputs from others.	A 'must' for any negotiator is the ability to understand where the other party is coming from. Being interpersonally sensitive via interpretation of body language and/or listening to subtle language cues, can reveal the other party's needs in terms of 'deal makers' and 'deal breakers'.
Influencing The ability to persuade others to change a viewpoint based on the understanding of their position and the recognition of the need to listen to this perspective and provide a rationale for change.	The ability to influence is recognised as a core competence for those needing to undertake negotiations. Regarded as a covert form of persuasion, it is essential during all phases of the negotiation process from stakeholder engagement through to implementation.
Intuitiveness Ability to arrive at a clear decision and drive their implementation when presented with incomplete or ambiguous information using both rational and 'emotional' or intuitive perceptions of key issues and implications.	Shown to have a significant correlation with the ability to influence, negotiators need good intuition in order to play in their negotiation tools at the appropriate time. Some persuasion methods such as Threat and Emotion are thought to need higher levels of intuition to deploy correctly.
Integrity Ability to display clear commitment to a course of action in the face of challenge and to match 'words and deeds' in encouraging others to support the chosen direction. The personal commitment to pursuing an ethical solution to a difficult business issue or problem.	Key when closing down the negotiation and undertaking ratification of the deal. Committing to the deal reached and ensuring implementation.

Figure 5.6   Elements of emotional intelligence

So what?

There is a dearth of empirical evidence supporting the soft skills required for negotiations. The Henley research provides a foundation for this based upon the premise of emotional intelligence, a concept that has gained increasing momentum among the academic community.

Taking the test can help individuals become aware of their own negotiation preferences together with any accompanying negotiation development needs.

Negotiation application

- Determining negotiator strengths and weaknesses.
- Assessing individual and team development needs.
- Highlighting behavioural requirements during the negotiation process.

Limitations

The concept is relatively new and needs further studies to promote its use on a wider basis. Some critics also suggest that the EQ test, which is based on self-perception, is insufficient on its own and should be used in conjunction with 360° feedback in order to gauge a broader view of the individual.

Further reading

You can read more about emotional intelligence in:

Dulewicz, S.V.D. and Higgs, M.J. (1998). *Emotional Intelligence: Managerial Fad or Valid Construct?* Henley Working Paper 9813. Henley Management College.
Goleman, D. (1996). *Emotional Intelligence: Why It Can Matter More than IQ.* London: Bloomsbury Publishing.
Reynolds, A. (2003). *Emotional Intelligence and Negotiation.* Hampshire: Tommo Press.

Associated templates

The following template can be used to assess potential procurement roles in relation to overall emotional intelligence score:

- Template 19: Emotional Intelligence.

20

INFLUENCING

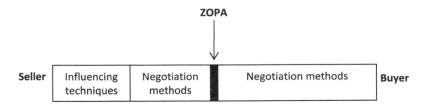

Figure 5.7 Influencing

Overview

Influencing is a form of negotiation; however, rather than exchange in order to agree, this process relies on subtle manipulation tactics. It is generally thought to be a covert and distributive approach to persuasion.

Two of the most noted academics in this area are Dr Robert B. Cialdini (2008) and Dr Gary Yukl (2012). Both have researched the subject in depth and have developed their own perspectives. Cialdini suggests there are six key influencing tactics while Yukl believes there are 11.

Elements

Yukl's and Cialdini's theories are outlined and compared in Figure 5.8:

Yukl	Cialdini
Rational Persuasion Using logic and evidence to support the discussion/argument. Example: 'It would be the most cost-effective method of production.'	
Inspirational Appeal Appealing to the other party's ideals, values and aspirations. Example: 'Ethically speaking, it would be the best approach.'	
Consultation Requesting participation/ideas and advice in order to achieve buy-in. Example: 'It's important that we understand what your view is so that we can take it into consideration.'	
Ingratiation Expressing respect for the other party generally and/or skills and expertise. Example: 'You have much more of an insight and understanding on this subject, it's good to see we agree.'	
Personal Appeal Using the favourable relationship between the parties to gain advantage. Example: 'We've been partners on this for some time and I know we could develop this situation to mutual benefit.'	**Liking** Likability used to engender trust and commitment. More likely to be influenced by an individual where there is rapport in existence. Example: 'It's great to see you again, I've missed our get togethers.'
Exchange Bargaining/trading of favours, promises, commitments and allegiances. Example: 'If you can give me your commitment to this program, then I can do the same with yours.'	**Reciprocity** Based on the principle of 'returning favours'. Uses the feeling of obligation to ensure a debt/favour is repaid. Example: 'You remember I managed to get your invoice paid on time? Well... do you think you could just get that product supplied a bit quicker?'
Coalition Creating a group of support to pressurise the lone party into submission. Example: 'The rest of the team agreed with me on that issue.'	**Social Proof** Sometimes referred to as 'following the crowd'. Assumes that if 'everyone is doing it', it must be right. Example: 'All of your competitors are buying the software upgrade, so you probably need to do the same.'

Figure 5.8   Yukl's and Cialdini's theories

Legitimating Using authority and/or chain of command to legitimise a position. Example: 'As the leading authority on this subject, I would suggest you don't debate this issue.'	**Authority** Uses chain of command/position/rules to influence those who are less powerful and/or knowledgeable. Example: 'The policies and procedures say you can't purchase this without my support.'
Pressure Threatening posture in order to gain compliance. Example: 'You need to buy into the decision, otherwise there could be trouble ahead.'	
Appraising Appealing to the other party's need for personal gain. Example: 'You could do well out of this, if you support the programme.'	
Collaboration Helping the other party through the provision of own resources. Example: 'We can help you to respond better by providing a consultant for a couple of days.'	
	Consistency If an individual behaves in a consistent vein then this can drive the behaviour of the other party to respond accordingly. Example: 'I will be double-checking your report, you know how I like to do that.'
	Scarcity Based on the principle that things are more attractive when availability is limited. Example: 'If you don't get that purchase order to me on time, the capacity will be gone.'

Figure 5.8   Continued

So what?

Sometimes it is better to influence rather than negotiate. A more covert approach may be less obvious and damaging to a relationship. Negotiation and influencing methods can be used together; however, the delineation between the two needs to be understood, so that they are not used inappropriately, at the wrong time or in contradiction to each other.

Influencing theory is often combined with stakeholder mapping, so that an effective and workable communication plan can be put in place.

Negotiation application

- Influencing rather than negotiation used primarily when dealing with internal stakeholders.
- Can be used as part of the conditioning process shortly before the negotiation takes place.
- A tailored strategy can be developed dependent upon the needs of the individual being influenced.
- Aids in rapport building and effective communication.

Limitations

Recent research has shown that influencing tactics tend to be used more frequently by those on the sales side rather than the buy side. It is thought that this is due to the need to 'soften up' the prospect prior to entering into the negotiation process itself. Therefore, it could be argued that influencing acts more as a pre-negotiation tool.

It is also posited that influencing is in fact manipulation and, therefore, could provoke an adverse response from the other party in the event that this is discovered.

Further reading

You can read more about influencing tactics in:

Yukl, G. (2012). *Leadership in Organizations.* 8th edition. Harlow: Pearson.
Cialdini, R.B. (2008). *Influence, Science and Practice.* 5th edition. Harlow: Pearson.

Associated templates

The following template can be used to assess influencing styles:

- Template 20: Influencing Styles Matrix.

PHASE 6

Closing the deal

Overview

Concluding the negotiation will require a calm approach, as it can often become quite tense and conflict-bound at this stage of the process.

It is useful to have some conversation control techniques and closing statements to hand, in order to draw the meeting to an orderly end. The final agreement should be captured and ratified, and both parties should feel satisfied with the resulting outcome, rather than 'played'.

This section concentrates on the role of the negotiator, and their need to take ownership when closing the deal. This way, the pace, recording and endpoint are shaped and influenced by them rather than the other party.

Figure 6.0   Phase 6: Closing the deal

21
THOMAS-KILMANN CONFLICT MODE INSTRUMENT

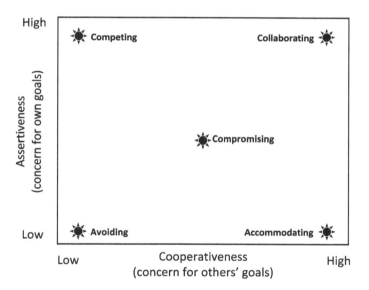

Figure 6.1 Thomas-Kilmann Conflict Mode Model

Source: Adapted from Ruble and Thomas (1976).

Overview

Initially conceived by Kenneth Thomas in the mid-1970s, he later joined forces with Ralph Kilmann and together they developed the Thomas-Kilmann Conflict Mode Instrument from which Figure 6.1 is a derivative.

The model looks at the five main ways of dealing with conflict in terms of assessing an individual's desire to achieve their goals compared to that of the other party.

It is thought that understanding one's own conflict style together with the other party's can help an individual adopt the best approach to a negotiation.

Elements

There are five main modes of conflict: Collaborating, Competing, Accommodating, Compromising and Avoiding. Conflict style is assessed by measuring one's assertiveness in relation to one's cooperativeness, as follows:

Competing – Assertive and uncooperative, the goal is to win. This style is often adopted when quick action and unpopular decisions are required or when there is leverage present. In a negotiation this may mean a win-lose approach.

Avoiding – Unassertive and uncooperative, the goal is to delay. This style is often adopted in order to deal with issues of little importance, to reduce tension or to buy time.

Collaborating – Assertive and cooperative, the goal is to work with other people in order to establish a win-win solution. This style is often adopted when integrating solutions, gaining commitment or improving relationships.

Accommodating – Unassertive and cooperative, the goal is to yield. This style is often adopted when showing reasonableness, developing performance and creating goodwill. In a negotiation this may mean a lose-win approach.

Compromising – Occupying the middle position, the goal is to find the middle ground and is often referred to as the 'let's make a deal' mode. In a negotiation this may mean that neither party wins outright if agreement is reached too quickly or alternatively that the end of a long negotiation has necessitated a compromise approach in order to reach a mutually satisfactory conclusion.

So what?

This is a well-recognised conflict profiling tool, which can aid awareness of individual style as well as provide a selection of alternative methods of engagement (in other words, the recognition of response will enable an adaptation of one's personal style to take place).

It is believed that the key to the successful utilisation of this approach to conflict is personal awareness, as failure to recognise one's own or others' styles could result in unsatisfactory resolution.

Negotiation application

- Supports the preparation for a negotiation with a supplier.
- Aids stakeholder management and communication.
- Facilitates negotiation project team meetings and the development of collaborative dynamics.

Limitations

This model assumes that individuals will be capable of switching between the various different styles depending upon the situation. However, human nature is such that in practice there is a habitual tendency to use only a limited number of them, and therefore success is limited to these.

From a negotiation perspective, it has also been argued that the 'compromise' style is merely a replication of 'accommodation', since both are reliant upon concession rather than assertion in order to move forward.

Further reading

You can read more about conflict theory and the work of Kenneth Thomas in:

Buchanan, D. and Huczynski, A. (2010). *Organizational Behaviour*. 7th edition. Harlow: Pearson.

Associated templates

The following template can be used to assess conflict styles:

• Template 21: Thomas–Kilmann Conflict Mode Instrument.

22

SUBLIMINAL LINGUISTICS

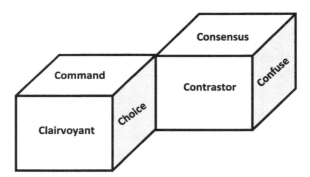

Figure 6.2 The Conversation Control Cube

Source: Adapted from Reynolds (2007).

Overview

Milton Erickson was an American psychiatrist specialising in medical hypnosis and family therapy. He was particularly noted for his approach to the unconscious mind and involvement in the development of the concept Neuro-Linguistic Programming (NLP).

Erickson believed that the unconscious mind was always listening and that, whether or not the patient was in a trance during his hypnosis consultations, suggestions using specific words could be made that had the potential to influence the individual.

His work was later adapted and built upon by the founders of NLP, Richard Bandler and John Grinder, who established a subliminal language structure designed principally with coaching and mentoring in mind. This has subsequently been used more widely in the commercial environment to persuade and influence and is often referred to as subliminal linguistics.

Elements

The Conversation Control Cube is a framework designed to help those in negotiation situations remember common linguistic mechanisms that work at an unconscious level. Sometimes the unconscious mind is also referred to as the subconscious – they are in essence the same.

Elements of the Cube

Command – Means Embedded Command. Commands are hidden/embedded within a sentence. The sentence is normally disguised by making it sound like a question.

Example: 'I think we *all agree* on that, don't we?'

Consensus – Means Universal Quantifier. Used to elicit consensus by suggesting that there is already a body of agreement in existence.

Example: '*Everyone* knows that's the right way forward.'

Contrastor – Means words like 'but' and 'however'. These words have a negative connotation, and therefore, it is better to change them to 'and' instead.

Example: 'That's a great piece of work, *and* this is how we can improve it' rather than 'That's a great piece of work, *but…*'.

Choice – Means Double Bind. This is used to promote the idea of choice when issuing an embedded command, when in fact there is none.

Example: '*You'll be signing* this contract *before or after* lunch?'

Confuse – Means Negative Suggestion. Commands are hidden/embedded within a sentence. The sentence is disguised, to sound as if you are asking the person to not do something. Negative suggestion works on the principle that the brain will focus on the command word.

Example: 'Don't *think* about looking at that aspect of the quotation.'

Clairvoyant – Means Mind Reader. Used to suggest similar/group thinking in order to build a body of agreement.

Example: 'I know that *Pat thinks the same* as I do on this matter.'

So what?

The advertising industry has been using subliminal messaging in marketing campaigns for many years, politicians use clever language structure in speech writing to persuade and evoke emotional responses in others and those in the commercial field use conversation control techniques to guide the negotiation process; for example, the Assumptive Closing technique is based on the Double Bind.

Understanding the power of language can help an individual to direct and manage a conversation. It is also useful to be able to recognise when such techniques are being used by another person on oneself. A popular counteraction method is as follows:

Acknowledge which conversation control technique is being used.

Break down the sentence and interpret meaning.
Challenge the meaning.

Negotiation application

- Supports more traditional negotiation tools and techniques.
- Can help to change the direction of a negotiation.
- Can provide a competitive edge in a negotiation.
- Aids awareness of use of conversation control techniques by other party.
- Increases individual negotiation linguistics repository.

Limitations

Erickson's work on hypnotism in his capacity as a psychiatrist was controversial during his lifetime and has remained so to the present day. Similarly, NLP trance theory has its dissenters. The central theme among critics is that there is a lack of scientific understanding when it comes to the unconscious brain. Research in the main is based on human responses rather than internal neural pathway responses. Although with the advent of MRI scanners, more empirical research is being conducted in this field.

It is also argued that in order to implant an embedded command into another person's sub-conscious, the subject should first be 'in the right state', i.e., calm, no defence barriers in place, willing to listen. This is often *not* the case during a negotiation.

Further reading

You can read more about the concept of subliminal linguistics in:

Silvester, T. (2012). *Word Weaving: A Comprehensive Guide to Creating Hypnotic Language.* Revised edition. Norwich: Quest Institute.
Charvet, S.R. (2010). *Words that Change Minds: Mastering the Language of Influence.* 2nd edition. Iowa: Kendall Hunt Publishing.
Weir, D.R. (2009). *The Way of Trance.* New York: New York Strategic Books.

Associated templates

The following template can be used to support the counteraction of subliminal linguistics:

- Template 22: Counteraction Template.

23

SUMMARISING AND RATIFICATION

Figure 6.3 Summarising and ratification

Overview

Summarising and ratification are key activities that support the closure of a negotiation and both are often overlooked. During the negotiation process it is important to build common ground and consensus with the other party. This helps establish confidence and trust with the other party and moves both positions closer to agreement.

Whilst consensus-building is at the heart of collaborative (integrative) negotiation, it is less so with competitive (distributive) negotiation. By using these simple techniques, more experienced negotiators move the points of discussion closer to agreement and remove elements of distrust and conflict.

Elements

There are three key techniques to consider, as shown in Figure 6.4.

Technique	What it is	When to use
Thank & Bank	Simple tactic of acknowledging movement and/or a concession from the other party, even if it is insufficient to satisfy your requirements. It has the effect of creating a 'milestone' in the progress of the negotiation – a reference point that can be returned to at a later point in the discussions if need be. This requires the lead negotiator to acknowledge the gesture from the other party (the 'thank') and then to pause the discussion so that a note can be made of the other party's concession (the 'bank'). The negotiation can then continue but if need be it can return to this point so that the concession is not lost.	Use this part-way through a negotiation each time there is a concession or a point of movement from the other party. It helps to encourage the other party and for them to know their offer has been acknowledged.
Summarising	Summarising is used to check the shared understanding of both parties and to build consensus at key stages through a negotiation discussion. Where there is a negotiation team, this can often be the role of the chairperson or lead negotiator. Summarising requires one party to repeat back a brief précis of what has been discussed and agreed (or not agreed) by both parties. If done accurately and without bias it will induce agreement from the other party and therefore act as a bridge-building behaviour. It also allows both parties to check understanding of the other and therefore to build trust and integrity in the negotiation process.	It is recommended to summarise only occasionally at critical points in the discussion. This will include key topic areas, individual commercial or technical issues, and should always be at the conclusion of a negotiation session.
Ratification	Ratification refers to the process of recording and formalising the agreement that has been reached at the end of a negotiation to ensure that it survives.	Informal ratification can take place in the form of shared note-taking, meeting minutes and/or e-mail exchange immediately at the end of the negotiation. These should always be made 'subject to contract'. Formal ratification involves conclusion of the negotiated outcome in the form of a contractual agreement or variation.

Figure 6.4   Summarising and ratification techniques

Each of these three techniques involves acknowledging the position reached with the other party in the negotiation and is designed to build consensus, shared understanding and common ground. This provides a platform to establish further agreement on outstanding matters.

So what?

Distrust and conflict often lie at the heart of negotiations and in order to reach a successful outcome these must be overcome. Each of these techniques provides a simple method of recognising and directly acknowledging to the other party progress within the negotiation.

The techniques are particularly relevant in individualistic cultures such as those found in Europe and North America, as they show an appreciation for the other party and therefore help to build bridges.

Negotiated outcomes that are not ratified can 'fall apart' when they start to be implemented. It is easy for the two parties to misinterpret the outcome and/or have slightly differing opinions on what was finally agreed. Ratification helps overcome any of these misunderstandings and therefore gives both parties confidence in the integrity of the agreement. Summarising and Thank & Bank also help achieve this same common understanding and help build an underpinning foundation to the final agreement.

Negotiation application

- Acknowledges a concession, compromise or movement from the other party.
- Confirms shared understanding of individual discussion points.
- Essential as part of the closure.
- Formalises the final agreement to ensure closure.
- Avoids misinterpretation and reopening the discussion.

Limitations

Some less experienced negotiators may consider techniques like Thank & Bank as signs of 'weakness' – i.e., that to acknowledge a concession from the other party is in some way to suggest interest or keenness and therefore to weaken one's position. However this is not the case, as a Thank & Bank or a summary can still be made while highlighting the areas of agreement and outstanding disagreement at the same time.

If one party continues to summarise the position repetitively, without any progress in the negotiation or movement from either party, then this can undermine the integrity of the discussion and can raise questions as to the willingness of that party to progress discussions.

Finally, when ratifying an outcome, it is imperative that neither party varies the points of agreement that have been reached. If this is done then it will undermine the agreement and could jeopardise any future discussions.

Further reading

You can read more about summarising and ratification in:

Lewicki, R.J., Barry, B. and Saunders, D.M. (2010). *Negotiation*. 6th edition. New York: McGraw-Hill.
Fells, R. (2010). *Effective Negotiation, from Research to Results*. Melbourne: Cambridge University Press.
Kennedy, G. (1998). *Kennedy on Negotiation*. Aldershot: Gower Publishing Ltd.

Associated templates

The following template can be used when summarising a negotiation:

- Template 23: Summary of Negotiation

24

GAME THEORY

Negotiator A		Negotiator B	
		Collaborate	Compete
	Collaborate	Compromise (sub-optimal outcome)	Lose-win
	Compete	Win-lose	Win-win (optimised outcome)

Figure 6.5   Game theory

Overview

Game theory is based on the use of mathematical modelling to recommend or predict actions that might be taken in order to maximise a competitive position. In the context of a negotiation, the negotiator's best course of action depends on what they expect the other party to do, which will have a direct affect upon the next 'move' they make.

There are two main branches of game theory; cooperative and non-cooperative. A cooperative game assumes that the players have full information and are able to form binding agreements, i.e., a legally binding contract, whereas a non-cooperative game deals largely with how individuals interact with one another in an effort to achieve their own goals in the absence of all the information, i.e., negotiation.

One of the best known examples used to illustrate the psychology behind game theory is the Prisoner's Dilemma.

Elements

The Prisoner's Dilemma is based on a once-off meeting where not all of the information is known – an uncooperative situation.

Scenario:

- Two suspects have been brought in for questioning, but the police have little evidence to convict either.
- The police need to talk to the suspects in order to get them to reveal more information which could lead to a conviction.
- The suspects are taken to separate rooms and offered the following choices:

  - Be the only one to confess and spend a maximum term of one year in prison.
  - If you both confess then it could mean four years each.
  - Stay quiet and face a possibility of eight years in prison (a conviction based on evidence provided by the other prisoner).
  - If you both stay quiet then we can still make a conviction, but it will only be for two years each.

A lack of facts, and not knowing how the other party will respond, can lead to a potentially disastrous outcome. Therefore, both suspects (players in the game) have to guess how the other will 'move'.

By translating the Prisoner's Dilemma into a negotiation setting using the Game Theory Negotiation Matrix, potential negotiator positions can be observed as shown in Figure 6.6

Collaborate/Collaborate	Both parties collaborate in the interests of reaching a compromise – parties do not optimise their relative positions.
Compete/Collaborate	One party wants to win at all costs and takes a very competitive position – leads to a win-lose outcome.
Collaborate/Compete	One party attempts to collaborate but the other party wants to compete – leads to a lose-win outcome.
Compete/Compete	Both negotiators take a competitive position – leads to a win-win optimised outcome.

Figure 6.6 Negotiator positions

So what?

Game theory can be a useful tool for analysing potential outcomes related to nego-tiation strategies; for example, a transactional ad hoc buyer/supplier relationship might only necessitate a once-off non-cooperative approach using a reverse auc-tion, while a long-term partnership might require a more cooperative, 'repeated-play' stance such as a cost down initiative resulting from a supplier relationship management programme.

Game theory specialists who have sophisticated mathematical software that can compute probable negotiation positions and outcomes can be used to assist in the running of negotiations. However, the costs involved can be prohibitive and so it is only worth doing for high value projects.

Negotiation application

- Can be used to analyse negotiation approaches.
- Supports the development of negotiation strategy.
- A useful model to help predict positions and outcomes prior to a negotiation.

Limitations

Although game theory is relatively simple to understand, it rests upon a number of more complicated assumptions such as, for example, that each party is seeking to maximise their outcome/each party is rational. Such parameters represent the ideal situation, which is difficult to replicate in a real-life terms.

Also, game theory focuses on a logical decision-making process and therefore ignores variables such as personality and experience. In particular, the notion of how an individual might act in the event that they have nothing to lose where behaviour can change dramatically has not been factored into the equation.

Finally, it should be noted that the introduction of game theory into long-term relationships could result in a lack of trust and ultimately affect the dynamics of the partnership.

Further reading

You can read more about game theory in:

Kennedy, G. (2003). *Perfect Negotiation.* 2nd edition. London: Random House Business Books.

Associated templates

The following template can be used to assess game theory outcomes:

- Template 24: Game Theory

PHASE 7

Implementing the deal

Overview

It is considered best practice to carry out an evaluation of the negotiation both from a procedural and individual standpoint. Self-reflection is thought to be one of the best ways to continuously improve performance. Learnings can then be shared among colleagues and, where appropriate, can contribute to the personal development planning process.

In the event that the agreement needs to be implemented across an international organisation, then it will also be necessary to understand the potential cultural issues that may arise.

This section looks at the final phase, and the factors that need to be considered when handing over the deal into a 'business as usual' (BAU) environment.

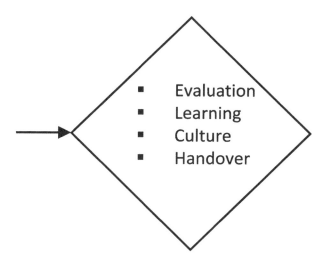

Figure 7.0   Phase 7: Implementing the deal

25

NEGOTIATION EVALUATION

Figure 7.1   Feedback mechanisms

Overview

Reflecting on negotiation performance is a powerful learning experience which considers past events and extracts valuable opportunities for continued improvement and development.

A thorough evaluation of the negotiation process can provide a 'parallel' journey of review, from which subsequent corrective action can be derived. It focuses on the content, process, outcomes and methodology applied, identifying both the positive elements and the potential areas for improvement.

Elements

When evaluating the success or otherwise of the negotiation process implemented by the project team or individual, techniques that could be included for measurement purposes are shown in Figure 7.2.

Feedback from peers/ key stakeholders	An informal or formal post-negotiation review meeting evaluating the overall process and encompassing internal customer satisfaction with outcomes, delivery and behaviours. The review can be extended to external stakeholders.
Outcomes versus goals	Analysis of the actual outcomes compared to desired outcomes or goals. What happened and why? What could be done differently or better next time? What learning, training or development methods will assist and facilitate change?
Use of BATNA	Assumes a BATNA is devised prior to the negotiation and used as a negotiation tactic. Was it successfully deployed? This can be linked to exploration of alternatives – was flexibility needed during the negotiation?
Critical incident analysis	Critical incidents, successful or unsuccessful, are analysed to establish what went right – or wrong – and what learning can be derived. This may be prepared in writing, as part of a personal development journal, or collectively via discussion with the negotiation team, or a coach or mentor in negotiation.
Monitoring post-negotiation behaviour/effectiven ess of contract in practice	Indicates the quality of the agreement reached on areas such as price, quality standards and delivery. Also considers the attitudes, satisfaction, commitment and compliance of both parties, and their stakeholders. These behaviours illustrate the 'state' of the relationship after the negotiation and if any 'repair' actions are necessary.

Figure 7.2 Techniques for measuring the negotiation process

So what?

Developing organisational negotiation capability is an iterative process. Capturing lessons learned centrally and disseminating among team members can help to incrementally improve overall performance.

Individual training needs may also be identified, which can help to inform a training and development plan accordingly.

Negotiation application

- Helps the negotiator to assess their strengths and weaknesses.
- Supports understanding of team development needs.
- Can aid the building of best practice negotiation format within the organisation.
- Can gain organisational competitive advantage through improved performance.

Limitations

Evaluation activities can be perceived negatively, provoking defensive behaviour instead of encouraging an open and positive learning experience. Success may depend on whether organisational culture provides a 'safe' environment to admit where potential failings or skill gaps exist. The ability to capture lessons learned and transfer the knowledge may be challenging. Understanding how to apply the learning for the good of the greater organisation may not be clear or straightforward.

Further reading

You can read more about negotiation evaluation in:

Kennedy, G. (2003). *Perfect Negotiation.* 2nd edition. London: Random House Business Books.
Lewicki, R.J., Barry, B. and Saunders, D.M. (2010). *Negotiation.* 6th edition. New York: McGraw-Hill.

Associated templates

The following template can be used to evaluate the negotiation:

- Template 25: Negotiation Process Evaluation.

26

KOLB'S EXPERIENTIAL LEARNING CYCLE

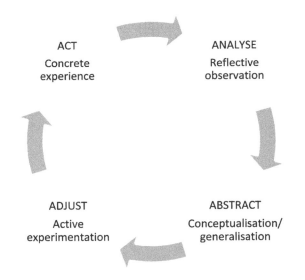

Figure 7.3   Kolb's experiential learning cycle

Overview

'Learning is the process whereby knowledge is created through the transformation of experience' (Kolb, 1984)

David A. Kolb's work is acknowledged by academics as seminal in the area of human learning behaviour. His learning cycle framework is comprised of four methods of learning that may be adopted by an individual.

Kolb views learning as an integrated process with each stage being mutually supportive of and feeding into the next. It is therefore possible to enter the cycle at any stage and follow it through its logical sequence. However, the theory posits that effective learning only occurs when an individual is able to execute all four stages of the model. Therefore, no one stage of the cycle is as effective as the entire learning process itself.

Elements

Effective learning occurs when an individual progresses through a cycle of four stages, as shown in Figure 7.4.

Learning	Description	Examples
Concrete experience	A new experience or situation is encountered, or a reinterpretation of an existing experience.	▪ Actively negotiating ▪ Problem-solving ▪ Discussion ▪ Trying out combinations of tactics.
Reflective observation	Of the new experience, of particular importance are any inconsistencies between experience and understanding.	▪ Ask for observation and feedback ▪ Write a short report on what took place ▪ Give feedback to other participants ▪ Quiet thinking time ▪ Tea and coffee breaks ▪ Completing learning logs or diaries.
Abstract conceptualisation	Reflection gives rise to a new idea, or a modification of an existing abstract concept.	▪ Suggest negotiation outcome scenarios ▪ Present models ▪ Give theories ▪ Give facts and then develop new hypothesis ▪ Research new ideas/areas of negotiation.
Active experimentation	The learner applies them to the world around them to see what results.	▪ Time to plan for next negotiation ▪ Use real-life case studies to practice on ▪ Include role play in training programmes ▪ Apply lessons learned internally to organisation.

Figure 7.4   Elements of Kolb's experiential learning cycle

So what?

Post-negotiation, it is important that individual learnings are captured and con-solidated. As a result of this exercise, a thorough personal development plan can be established, with specific needs being met by a tailored blended learning programme.

Self-reflection in particular, carried out immediately post-event, is thought to be one of the most valuable ways of continually improving performance.

A popular opinion among negotiation authors is that good negotiators are never satisfied with their performance, as they feel they could always have achieved more upon reflection.

Negotiation application

- Support others with their personal development planning in relation to nego-tiation needs.
- Identifying own learning preferences and sourcing ways to build capability.
- Increases overall organisational negotiation capability as part of a planned training needs analysis process.

Limitations

While the theory is good at analysing how learning occurs for individuals, it does not take into account learning that occurs in larger social groups, i.e., how does the individual's interaction with a larger group impact the experiential learning process?

Also, critics argue that learning styles may not be stable over time. For example, one study has found that age can affect an individual's preference for reflective learning; for example, the older you are, the more likely it is that reflective learning will take place.

Further reading

You can read more about experiential learning theory in:

Kolb, D.A. (1984). *Experiential Learning Experience as a Source of Learning and Development.* New Jersey: Prentice Hall.
Boud, D., Keogh, R. and Walker, D. (1985). *Reflection: Turning Experience in to Learning.* London: Kogan Page.

Associated template

The following template can be used to assess personal negotiation performance:

- Template 26: Personal Negotiation Evaluation.

27

CULTURAL DIMENSIONS

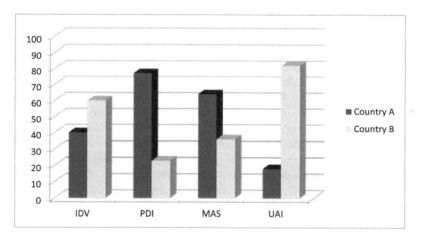

Figure 7.5 Cultural comparison graph

Overview

International negotiation can be fraught with difficulties due to cultural, language and time zone barriers. Geert Hofstede (2003), a Dutch researcher, developed a framework for cross-cultural communication in the early 1970s based on 100,000 questionnaires completed by IBM employees across the globe. From this, Hofstede was able to quantify observable differences between cultures. This has subsequently become known as his '5 dimensions' theory and is still regarded as seminal today.

Elements

Hofstede's original work looked at four cultural dimensions, i.e., a continuum approach with an opposing societal value at each end. A fifth dimension was added in the early 1990s as a result of additional research carried out in conjunction with the Chinese. The dimensions are as follows:

Power Distance Index (PDI) – Looks at how society views the distribution of power and the extent to which power distribution is accepted; for example, cultures that have low PDI scores are seen as democratic and consultative, whereas those with high PDI scores are viewed as autocratic, paternalistic and hierarchical.

Individualism (IDV) – This dimension looks at how individualistic a culture/society may be; for example, do people see themselves as part of a collective (a low score), or as individuals fending for themselves or competing against one another (a high score)?

Uncertainty Avoidance Index (UAI) – Looks at a society's tolerance for uncertainty or ambiguity; for example, people in societies with a high score tend to be more emotional and deal with this by enforcing rules and procedures in order to mitigate risk, where those in a society with a low score are happier with unstructured situations and change and are viewed as more pragmatic.

Masculinity (MAS) – This dimension looks at whether a society is more masculine or feminine in nature; for example, masculine cultures tend to value competitiveness, assertiveness and materialism, whereas feminine cultures place more value on relationships and quality of life. Also, in masculine cultures the difference between gender roles is more obvious.

Long term Orientation (LTO) – The fifth dimension to be added was initially called 'Confucian Dynamism', describing how societies view time. Those that have a preference for long-term orientation are more concerned with the future, while those with a short time horizon focus on past and present events; for example, tradition, fulfilment of social obligations and so on.

It should be noted that in 2010 a sixth dimension, **Indulgence**, was included, looking at the need for a society to satisfy needs immediately or restrain from doing so. Data is still in the process of being collated for this area.

So what?

There is a wealth of information relating to Hofstede's work and how it may be used from a negotiation perspective. Country scores (can be found on Hofstede's website – www.geerthofstede.nl) have also been found to correlate with other country specific data; for example, the Power Distance Index correlates with income inequality, Individualism has been linked to national wealth and high scores in relation to Masculinity correlate with a low percentage of women in democratically elected governments.

Hofstede's framework enables a basic understanding of cultural dimensions that can increase success in negotiations and reduce the potential for frustration and conflicts.

Negotiation application

- Enhances the international negotiation process.
- Aids communication between the parties.
- Can provide a competitive edge in a negotiation.
- Helps to avoid misunderstandings and potential conflict.

Limitations

One of the biggest critiques of Hofstede's work revolves around the sample. Although 100,000 questionnaires from more than 70 countries were completed, thus providing a significant pool of data, the fact remains that participants were extracted from one source only – IBM, which could have skewed the results. Others argue that it is this commonality that allowed Hofstede to focus on country rather than organisational culture patterns.

Hofstede himself stresses that the cultural dimensions are only a framework to help assess a given culture and thus provide for better decision-making. There are other factors to take into consideration such as personality, family history and personal wealth. The proposed dimensions cannot predict individual behaviours and do not take into account individual personalities.

Further reading

You can read more about the impact of culture on negotiation in:

Hofstede, G. (2003). *Culture's Consequences: Comparing Values, Behaviours, Institutions and Organizations Across Nations.* 2nd edition. Beverly Hills CA: Sage Publications.
Hofstede, G., Hofstede, G.J. and Minkov, M. (2010). *Cultures and Organisations: Software of the Mind: Intercultural Cooperation and its Importance for Survival.* 3rd edition. New York: McGraw-Hill.
Schein, E.H. (2010). *Organizational Culture and Leadership.* 4th edition. San Francisco, CA: Jossey-Bass.

Associated template

The following template can be used to review cultural differences that could impact a negotiation:

- Template 27: Cultural Difference Assessment Template

28

HANDOVER AND CONTRACT MANAGEMENT

Figure 7.6 Three levels of contract management

Overview

The negotiation process is not over once the deal has been completed. Implementation will mean much discussion with internal and external stakeholders alike.

It is necessary to consider the length and complexity of the contract and the ongoing issues that may occur such as agreeing performance measurement criteria and prices for goods/services outside of the original specification, aspects that may not have been included within the initial agreement.

To aid a smooth transition into a 'business as usual' (BAU) environment, the negotiator must ensure that an appropriate handover document including a detailed contract management plan is instituted.

Elements

There are three levels of contract management that could be implemented:

Relationship management

This is commonly regarded as the pinnacle or apex of contract management, and focuses on managing the relationship for the long term, the aim being smarter working and a philosophy of continuous improvement. Not all agreements will necessitate such an approach, usually only those that are regarded as vital/key to the business, but those that do may exhibit the following characteristics:

- Long-term partnerships
- Risk in the supply chain
- Difficult market dynamics
- Joint vision and goals
- High value.

Such agreements would also include performance management.

Performance management

Performance management concentrates on 'managing to contract', ensuring that what was agreed by both parties is implemented. Measurement tools and techniques like Service Level Agreements (SLAs) and Key Performance Indicators (KPIs) will help to drive this process. There will be a far larger number of suppliers that will need to adopt this methodology. For those deploying this approach only (i.e., not important or vital enough to include relationship management) they may exhibit the following characteristics:

- Long-term agreement
- Some difficulty in the marketplace
- High level of performance necessary
- Outsourced arrangement.

Service delivery

Service delivery is where implementation is carried out at 'shop floor' level, i.e., between those delivering/consuming the product and therefore contract management relies upon the working relationship between the individuals concerned. In the event of disputes/need for negotiation, it may be that these are escalated to those involved in either performance or relationship management.

So what?

A clear and concise handover document that stipulates how the deal is to be implemented and managed is essential if maximum value is to be derived from the agreement negotiated.

Assessing the level of resource required to undertake the handover is an important part of the process. It should be remembered that each deal will vary in magnitude and therefore an effort versus reward equation will need to be made accordingly.

Developing a clear way forward also allows internal stakeholders to contribute to the plan, and therefore gains buy-in, which should make proceedings less contentious and conflict bound.

Negotiation application

- Helps to provide a structure for ongoing negotiations, i.e., who is responsible for agreeing pricing in the long term.
- Guarantees that what has been negotiated is delivered.
- Ensures that implantation issues aren't brushed under the carpet.
- Provides an opportunity for stakeholders to buy-in to the deal agreed and to escalate issues during implementation.

Limitations

Implementing a deal can vary in difficulty depending upon the scale and complexity of the contract. It is not uncommon for organisations to underestimate the level of manpower required, especially when there are other projects competing for the same resources. Equally, it should be remembered that not all agreements need close management, and therefore the key is to correctly identify the type of management effort required at the outset. This would involve deploying a further detailed segmentation framework in order to assist the process.

Further reading

You can read more about handover and contract management in:

Cummins, T., David, M. and Kawamoto, K. (2011). *Contract and Commercial Management: The Operational Guide*. Zaltbommel: Van Haren Publishing.

Associated template

The following template can be used to assess the level of negotiation required for contract management:

- Template 28: Contract Management Effort.

Templates

Strategy Adoption Matrix

High

Hybrid	Integrative
Distributive	Win/Perceived Win

Difficulty of Market

Low　　　　　　　　　　**Relationship**　　　　　　　　**High**

A review of market difficulty and the relationship between the parties will help to identify a suitable negotiation strategy.

Negotiation Roles

Role	Details
Chairperson	
Lead Negotiator	
Support Negotiator	
Technical Expert	
Observer/Note Taker	

Negotiation Agenda Checklist

Structure	
Who is attending?	
Any introductions, by whom?	
Areas to be discussed	
Who will summarise the position?	
Who will wrap up and close?	
Location	
Home	
Away	
Room Ergonomics	
Seating plan	
Table size	
Table shape	
Chair arrangement	
Availability of refreshments	
Use of mobile phones	
Provision of presentation equipment	
Additional breakout areas	
Timings	
Start time (fixed)	
Finish time (fixed)	
Breakout session times (fixed)	
Factors to take into consideration	
Agenda Item Positioning	
Will big ticket items be discussed early on or held back?	

© 2019 Andrea Cordell

Negotiation SWOT

Strengths	**Weaknesses**	Internal Factors
Opportunities	**Threats**	External Factors

Beneficial Factors   Detrimental Factors

Building Rapport

Pushover	**Respect**
No incentive to participate	**Begrudging movement**

Rapport

Low   Negotiation Capability   **High**

Source: Adapted from Reynolds (2003)

© 2019 Andrea Cordell

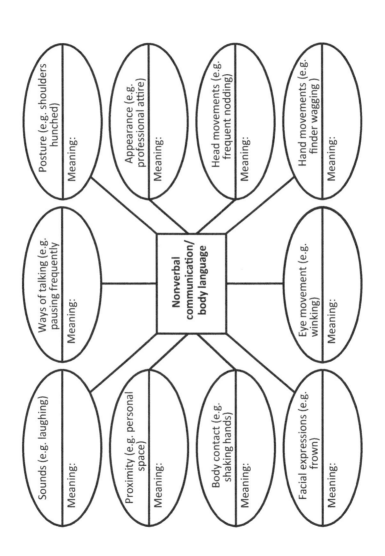

Posture (e.g. shoulders hunched)

Meaning:

Appearance (e.g. professional attire)

Meaning:

Head movements (e.g. frequent nodding)

Meaning:

Hand movements (e.g. finder wagging)

Meaning:

Ways of talking (e.g. pausing frequently

Meaning:

Non-verbal communication/ body language

Eye movement (e.g. winking)

Meaning:

Sounds (e.g. laughing)

Meaning:

Proximity (e.g. personal space)

Meaning:

Body contact (e.g. shaking hands)

Meaning:

Facial expressions (e.g. frown)

Meaning:

NLP Self-Assessment Test

1. **When you contact people, do you prefer:**

   a) Meeting face to face?

   b) Talking on the telephone?

   c) Getting together to share an activity (walking, sports, etc.)?

2. **What do you notice most about people in general?**

   a) How they look or dress

   b) How they sound when they talk

   c) How they stand or move

3. **What is the best way for you to learn?**

   a) See someone demonstrate what to do

   b) Get verbal instructions

   c) Get 'hands-on' experience

4. **What do you do when you get angry?**

   a) Clench your fists, grit your teeth, storm off

   b) Shout and let everyone know about it

   c) Go very quiet and perhaps seethe inwardly

5. **When in conversation with others, do you:**

    a) Use a lot of gestures?

    b) Enjoy listening but get impatient to talk?

    c) Dislike either talking or listening for too long?

6. **When you have many things to do, do you:**

    a) Make lists for yourself or imagine doing them?

    b) Keep reminding yourself that you have things to do?

    c) Feel uncomfortable until all or most of the things are done?

7. **When you are reading, do you:**

    a) Enjoy descriptive passages, imagine scenes clearly?

    b) Enjoy dialogue, hear characters speaking?

    c) Prefer action stories, or tend not to read much?

8. **What do you tend to memorise?**

    a) Forget names but remember faces

    b) Remember names, words and numbers

    c) Remember best the things you've done

9. **When you have leisure time, do you prefer to:**

    a) Watch TV, a video or go to the movies?

    b) Listen to music, radio or read books?

    c) Do something physical, or athletic?

10. **What would make you suspect that someone was lying to you?**

    a) The way they look or avoid looking at you

    b) Their tone of voice

    c) A feeling you get about their sincerity

11. **I can tell what another person is thinking by:**

    a) The look of their face

    b) The tone of their voice

    c) The vibes I get from them

12. **When I'm in a restaurant reading a menu and trying to decide what to order, I would:**

    a)   Visualise the food

    b)   Discuss with myself the various options

    c)   Read the list and choose what feels best

13. **I let other people know how I am feeling by:**

    a)   The clothes I dress in and the way I do my hair

    b)   The tone of my voice, sighs and other sounds

    c)   My body posture and gestures

14. **When I meet an old friend whom I haven't seen for some time, I would normally say:**

    a)   It's great to see you again

    b)   It's great to hear your voice again

    c)   I've missed you! (and give them a big hug)

15. **I tend to naturally say things like:**

    a)   I see what you mean

    b)   That sounds sensible to me

    c)   I have a good feeling for that

16. **When I have to decide upon something important, I tend to:**

    a)   See all aspects of the situation

    b)   Justify the decision to myself and/or somebody else

    c)   Know when it's the right decision because my gut feelings tell me so

Score

Mostly As – Visual

Mostly Bs – Auditory

Mostly Cs – Kinaesthetic

Eye Accessing
Observation Sheet

Question Prompt	Observed reaction	Classic reaction
What does Prince William look like on TV? (visual remembered)	◯ ◯	👁 👁
Picture a black and white rabbit (visual construct)	◯ ◯	👁 👁
Imagine Mickey Mouse saying your name and address (auditory construct)	◯ ◯	👁 👁
What do you say to yourself when you are really pleased with something? (internal dialogue)	◯ ◯	👁 👁
What was the first thing you said at work this morning? (auditory remembered)	◯ ◯	👁 👁
Put yourself into their shoes (feelings)	◯ ◯	👁 👁
Which way do you turn a key in a lock? (feelings)	◯ ◯	👁 👁
How do your two favourite groups sound when they are mixed together? (auditory create)	◯ ◯	👁 👁

© 2019 Andrea Cordell

Template

9

Questioning Techniques

Question	Type	Action	Outcome

BATNA

Variable (e.g., discount, lead times)	Importance Rating (1 being most important, 5 being least important)	BATNA	Negotiated Position	Decision

Template

11

ZOPA

Their Position	ZOPA	Our Position	Variable

Negotiation Goals and Targets

Target	Description	Value

Tradeables and
Straw Issues

Variables for us:	Perceived variables of the other party:

First Offer

	100% Walk Away (Insult)	50/50 (Extreme)	100% Continue (Credible)	Agree Next Move (Reasonable)	ZOPA		

Negotiation Power

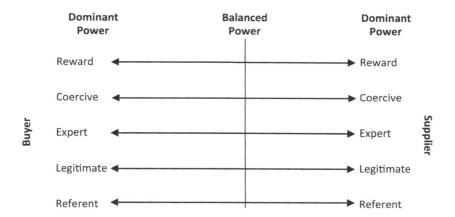

Dominant Power	Balanced Power	Dominant Power
Reward		Reward
Coercive		Coercive
Expert		Expert
Legitimate		Legitimate
Referent		Referent

Buyer

Supplier

Compare the power between the two parties, and annotate which one has the most along each continuum.

Personality and Negotiation Self-Assessment Guide

based on Myers Briggs typology

Big Thinker (ENTP):	Counsellor (INFJ):	Go-getters (ESTP):	Ideologists (INFP):
Likes: Talking, looking for opportunities and tackling problems head on Dislikes: routine Can sometimes appear abrupt and challenging. *Preferred negotiation tool: Logic*	Likes: developing insights, helping others reach their potential and privacy Dislikes: crowds and working with many others Can sometimes appear difficult to get to know. *Preferred negotiation tool: Compromise*	Likes: being Inventive, resourceful problem solvers, new challenges Dislikes: rules and routine Can sometimes appear very determined, verging on stubborn. *Preferred negotiation tool: Bargaining*	Likes: being alone, led by their heart Dislikes: making clinical decisions Can sometimes appear stubborn, especially around their values system. *Preferred negotiation tool: Bargaining*
Innovators (ENFP):	**Leaders (ENTJ):**	**Masterminds (INTJ):**	**Mentors (ENFJ):**
Likes: flexible work arrangements, creative environments and like to think of themselves as imaginative, sociable and sympathetic Dislikes: rules and procedures Can sometimes appear rebellious and unstructured. *Preferred negotiation tool: Emotion*	Likes: strategy, the 'big picture' and discussing complex issues to spark a debate Dislikes: detailed analysis and being micromanaged Can sometimes appear uncaring and bullish. *Preferred negotiation tool: Threat*	Likes: being future orientated, logical decision making and working independently Dislikes: inefficiency Can sometimes appear very focused and individualistic rather than a team player. *Preferred negotiation tool: Logic*	Likes: working with others, developing capability and bringing people together Dislikes: criticism by boss and peers Can sometimes appear oversensitive. *Preferred negotiation tool: Compromise*

Nurturers (ISFJ):	Peacemaker (ISFP):	Performers (ESFP):	Providers (ESFJ):
Likes: family values, harmony and consensus Dislikes: arguments and confrontation Can sometimes appear to have difficulty making decisions if it means hurting someone's feelings. *Preferred negotiation tool:* *Compromise*	Likes: personal freedom, and being sensitive to the feelings of others Dislikes: discord Can sometimes appear weak in the working environment rather than just naturally quiet. *Preferred negotiation tool:* *Compromise*	Likes: being surrounded by people and building rapport with others Dislikes: working alone and being cornered into making a final decision Can sometimes appear overly chatty. *Preferred negotiation tool:* *Emotion*	Likes: loyalty, order, tradition and following through on commitments Dislikes: solo working Can sometimes appear uncomfortable with radical change. *Preferred negotiation tool:* *Compromise*
IResolvers ISTP):	**Realists (ISTJ):**	**Supervisors (ESTJ):**	**Strategists (INTP):**
Likes: getting to the heart of a problem, quickly finding a solution, making rational decisions Dislikes: Discussing problems through with others Can appear to focus on short-term results and lose sight of the big picture. *Preferred negotiation tool:* *Bargaining/Emotion*	Likes: process and procedures, are steady workers who meet deadlines. Dislikes: thinking of how other people are feeling when making decisions Can sometimes appear too logical or tough-minded. *Preferred negotiation tool:* *Logic*	Likes: bringing order to the work place, and working on clear achievable goals Dislikes: instability and ambiguity Can sometimes appear irritated when those around them don't follow procedure. *Preferred negotiation tool:* *Logic*	Likes: being quiet, curious, easy going Dislikes: dealing with practical issues such as resources and budget Can sometimes appear overly procedural. *Preferred negotiation tool:* *Logic*

Source: Adapted from research by Reynolds (2008)

Persuasion Methods

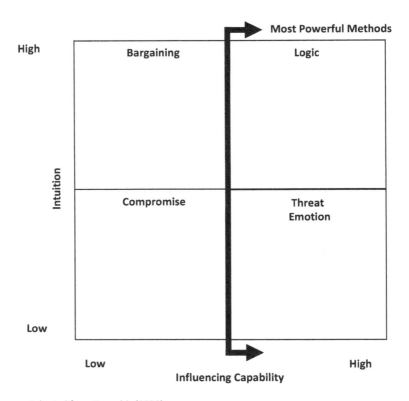

Source: Adapted from Reynolds (2003).

© 2019 Andrea Cordell

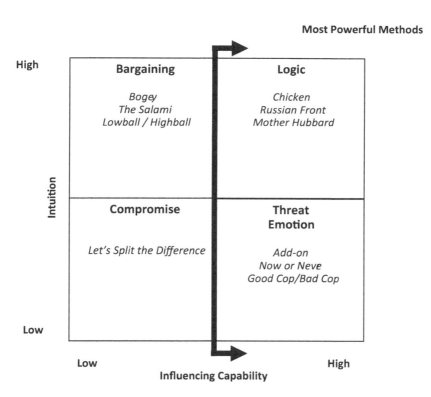

Most Powerful Methods

	Bargaining	**Logic**
High	*Bogey*	*Chicken*
	The Salami	*Russian Front*
	Lowball / Highball	*Mother Hubbard*
	Compromise	**Threat Emotion**
	Let's Split the Difference	*Add-on*
		Now or Neve
Low		*Good Cop/Bad Cop*

Intuition

Low   High

Influencing Capability

Source: Adapted from Reynolds (2003).
A review of tactics in relation to persuasion methods.

Emotional Intelligence

High

Procurement Management	Leader
Ineffective Buyer	Effective 'wheeler dealer'

Overall EI

Low   **Negotiation Capability**   High

Source: Adapted from Reynolds (2003)

© 2019 Andrea Cordell

Quadrant	Definition	Current Profile	Development Potential
Leader	Ability to navigate the organisation successfully, lead and manage people through inspiring vision.	Director/head of procurement/CPO (Chief Procurement Officer)	Board member
Procurement management	Good overall management skills with development needs around influencing and negotiation.	Senior procurement managers/ procurement management	Director/head of procurement
Effective 'wheeler dealer'	Good negotiation skills with development needs around softer skills associated with man management.	Buyer/senior buyer	Possible career cul de sac
Ineffective Buyer	Low capability both from a managerial and functional perspective.	Graduate/junior buyer/buyer	Buyer/senior buyer

Template 20 — Influencing Styles Matrix

High

Non-confrontational Adaptive/Flexible Win-Perceived Win Approach Intuitive Barter/Trader Style	Politically Adept Flexible Confrontational Win-Perceived Win Approach Subtle Manipulation Style
Non-confrontational Untrained Politically Inept Win-Win Approach (or both lose a little) Anyone Can Negotiate Style	Articulate in Argument Confrontatonal Facts and Data Win-Perceived Win Approach Reasoning Style

Intuition

Low   **Influencing**   **High**

Source: Adapted from Reynolds (2003)

P   © 2019 Andrea Cordell

Thomas-Kilmann Conflict Mode Instrument

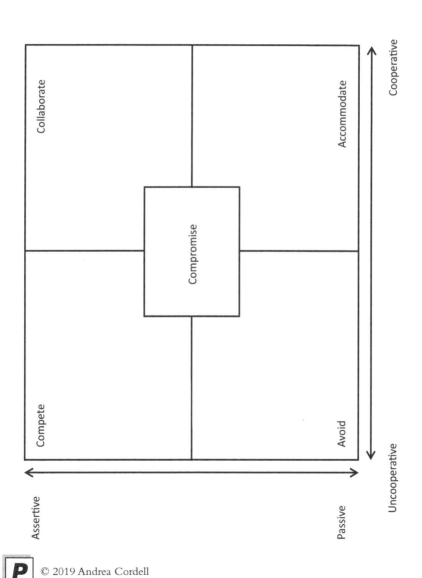

Counteraction Template

Conversation Control Technique	A	B	C

Source: Adapted from Reynolds (2007).

A = Acknowledge

B = Breakdown

C = Challenge

Template	
23	**Summary of Negotiation**

Variable	Negotiated Position	Outstanding Points to be Agreed	Action /Owner	Reflection
				☺ ☺
				☺ ☺
				☺ ☺
				☺ ☺
				☺ ☺
				☺ ☺
				☺ ☺

P © 2019 Andrea Cordell

Template **24** | **Game Theory**

		Negotiator B	
		Collaborate	**Compete**
Negotiator A	**Collaborate**	*Compromise (sub-optimal outcome)*	*Lose-Win*
	Compete	*Win-Lose*	*Win-Win (optimised outcome)*

Negotiation Process Evaluation

Team		Date	
Category			
Original tasks	Ideal		
	Optimal		
	Fall-back		
Actual outcome			
Areas in which the team could have improved			
Areas in which we achieved goals and/or did well			
Things we would do differently next time			

Personal Negotiation Evaluation

	Date			
Name				
STOP Key things that I need to stop doing... now				
HOLD Key things that I need to continue to do, just as I am already				
START Key things that I need to start doing... now				

Cultural Difference Assessment Template

Example/description	Impact on negotiation	Action required
1. Time ▪ In many Asian countries the perception of time is past-oriented (ancestors, values). ▪ In Latin American countries as well as Southern European countries time is present-oriented. ▪ In Western Europe as well as North America time is future-oriented (vision, what's on the horizon, planning).		
2. Head Shaking ▪ Shaking the head in a horizontal direction in most countries means 'no', while in most parts of India it means 'yes'.		
3. Thumbs Up ▪ Showing the thumb held upwards can mean 'everything is OK' in most parts of Europe and America, while in some Islamic countries as well as Sardinia and Greece it could be interpreted as a rude sexual sign.		
4. Pausing/Silence ▪ In North America as well as in Arabic countries, pauses between words are usually short. While in Japan long pauses can give certain meaning to some spoken words.		

▪ Enduring silence is perceived as comfortable in Japan, whereas in Europe and North America it may cause insecurity and embarrassment. Scandinavians, by Western standards, are more tolerant of silence during conversations.		
5. Laughing ▪ Laughing is associated in most countries with happiness, whereas in Japan it can be a sign of confusion/embarrassment.		
6. Interpretation of the word 'compromise' ▪ In the UK, Ireland and Commonwealth countries, the word 'compromise' has a positive meaning, i.e., an agreement where both parties win something; whereas in the USA it may have negative connotations (as both parties lose something).		
7. Social Setting ▪ In Mediterranean European countries, Latin America and Sub-Saharan Africa, it is normal, or at least widely tolerated, to arrive half an hour late for a dinner invitation, whereas in Germany and Switzerland this could be interpreted as extremely rude.		
8. Greetings ▪ In Africa, saying to a female friend one has not seen for a while that she has put on weight means she is physically healthier than before, whereas this would be considered as an insult in Europe, North America and Australia.		
9. Business Etiquette ▪ In Japan it is extremely important to study a business card once it has been proffered by a visitor. In Western Europe and America this is seen as less vital to the commencement of business proceedings.		

Hofstede Cultural Dimensions Scores:
US: IDV ☐
          PDI ☐
          MAS ☐
          UAI ☐
	Hofstede Cultural Dimensions Scores:
	THEM: IDV ☐
	             PDI ☐
	             MAS ☐
	             UAI ☐	

Contract Management Effort

Template **28**

Contract Management Categorisation

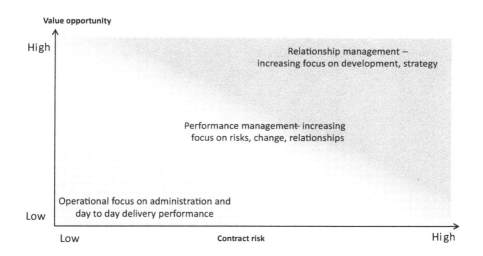

Value opportunity

High — Relationship management –
increasing focus on development, strategy

Performance management– increasing
focus on risks, change, relationships

Operational focus on administration and
day to day delivery performance

Low

Low — Contract risk — High

© 2019 Andrea Cordell

BIBLIOGRAPHY
AND SUGGESTED FURTHER
READING

Bandler, R. and Grinder, J. (1981). *Frogs into Princes: Neuro Linguistic Programming*. 1st edition. USA: Real People Press.

Berrien, F.K. (1944). *Practical Psychology*. New York: Macmillan.

Boddy, D. and Paton, S. (2010). *Management: An Introduction*. 5th edition. Harlow: Prentice Hall.

Borg, J. (2013). *Body Language: How to Know What's REALLY Being Said*. 3rd edition. Harlow: Pearson.

Boud, D., Keogh, R. and Walker, D. (1985). *Reflection: Turning Experience in to Learning*. London: Kogan Page.

Brown, J.M., Berrien, F.K., Russell, D.L. and Wells, W.D. (1966). *Applied Psychology*. New York: Macmillan.

Buchanan, D. and Huczynski, A. (2010). *Organizational Behaviour*. 7th edition. Harlow: Pearson.

Chamoun-Nicolas, H. and Hazlett, R.D. (2007). *Negotiate like a Phonenician: Discover Tradeables*. Houston: Key-Negotiations.

Charvet, S.R. (2010). *Words that Change Minds: Mastering the Language of Influence*. 2nd edition. Iowa: Kendall Hunt Publishing.

Cialdini, R.B. (2007). *Influence: The Psychology of Persuasion*. Revised edition. New York: HarperBusiness.

Cialdini, R.B. (2008). *Influence, Science and Practice*. 5th edition. Harlow: Pearson.

Cordell, A. and Thompson, I. (2018). *The Procurement Models Handbook*. 3rd edition. London: Routledge.

Cummins, T., David, M. and Kawamoto, K. (2011). *Contract and Commercial Management: The Operational Guide*. Zaltbommel: Van Haren Publishing.

Dulewicz, S.V.D. and Higgs, M.J. (1998). *Emotional Intelligence: Managerial Fad or Valid Construct?* Henley Working Paper 9813. Henley Management College.

Fells, R. (2010). *Effective Negotiation, from Research to Results*. Melbourne: Cambridge University Press.

Fisher, R. and Ury, W. (1997). *Getting to Yes: Negotiating an Agreement Without Giving In*. 2nd edition. London: Random House Business.

Fisher, R., Ury, W. and Patton, B. (1982). *Getting to Yes: Negotiating an Agreement Without Giving In*. 1st edition. London: Hutchinson Paperback.

French, J. and Raven, B. (1959). The bases of social power. In *Studies in Social Power*, D. Cartwright (ed.), pp. 150–167. Ann Arbor, MI: Institute for Social Research.

Galinsky, A. and Musseriler, T. (2010). First offers as anchors: the role of perspective-taking and negotiator focus. *Journal of Personality and Social Psychology*, 81(4), 657–669.

Goleman, D. (1996). *Emotional Intelligence: Why It Can Matter More than IQ.* London: Blooms-bury Publishing.

Greenhalgh, L. (2001). *Managing Strategic Relationships: The Key to Business Success.* New York: The Free Press.

Hofstede, G. (2003). *Culture's Consequences: Comparing Values, Behaviours, Institutions and Organizations Across Nations.* 2nd edition. Beverly Hills CA: Sage Publications.

Hofstede, G., Hofstede, G.J. and Minkov, M. (2010). *Cultures and Organisations: Software of the Mind: Intercultural Cooperation and its Importance for Survival.* 3rd edition. New York: McGraw-Hill.

Johnson, G., Scholes, K. and Whittington, R. (2010). *Exploring Strategy: Text and Cases.* 9th edition. Harlow: Prentice Hall.

Jung, C.G. (1971). *Psychological Types (Collected works of C.G. Jung, Volume 6).* 3rd edition. Princeton, NJ: Princeton University Press. First appeared in German in 1921.

Karrass, C.L. (1993). *The Negotiation Game: How to Get What You Want.* 2nd edition. New York: HarperBusiness.

Kennedy, G. (1998). *Kennedy on Negotiation.* Aldershot: Gower Publishing Ltd.

Kennedy, G. (2003). *Perfect Negotiation.* 2nd edition. London: Random House Business Books.

Kolb, D.A. (1984). *Experiential Learning Experience as a Source of Learning and Development.* New Jersey: Prentice Hall.

Lax, D.A. and Sebenius, J.K. (1986). *The Manager as Negotiator: Bargaining for Cooperation and Competitive Gain.* New York: The Free Press.

Lewicki, R.J., Barry, B. and Saunders, D.M. (2010). *Essentials of Negotiation.* 6th edition. London: McGraw-Hill.

Locke, E.A. and Latham, G.P. (1984). *Goal Setting: A Motivational Technique That Works.* Harlow: Prentice Hall.

Lysons, K. and Farrington, B. (2012). *Purchasing and Supply Chain Management.* 8th edition. Harlow: Pearson.

Mehrabian, A. (1972). *Silent Messages: Implicit Communication of Emotions and Attitudes.* California: Wadsworth Publishing Co Inc.

Myers-Briggs, I. (2000). *Introduction to Type.* 6th edition. Revised edition by L.K. Kirby and K.D. Myers. California: CPP Inc.

Nierenberg, G.I. (1987). *The Fundamentals of Negotiating.* Reprint edition. New York: Hawthorn Books.

Rackham, N. (1996). *The SPIN Selling Fieldbook: Practical Tools, Methods, Exercises and Resources.* New York: McGraw-Hill Professional.

Ready, R. and Burton, K. (2015). *Neuro-Linguistic Programming for Dummies.* 3rd edition. West Sussex: John Wiley & Sons Ltd.

Reynolds, A. (2003). *Emotional Intelligence and Negotiation.* Hampshire: Tommo Press.

Reynolds, A. (2007). Motivational speech. *Supply Management,* June, 34.

Reynolds, A. (2008). What are you like? *Supply Management: Guide to Procurement,* September, 19.

Ruble, T.L. and Thomas, K.W. (1976). Support for a two-dimensional model for conflict behavior. *Organizational Behavior and Human Performance,* 16, 143–155.

Schein, E.H. (2010). *Organizational Culture and Leadership.* 4th edition. San Francisco, CA: Jossey-Bass.

Silvester, T. (2012). *Word Weaving: A Comprehensive Guide to Creating Hypnotic Language.* Revised edition. Norwich: Quest Institute.

Thompson, L., Peterson, E. and Brodt, S.E. (1996). Team negotiations: an examination of integrative and distributive bargaining. *Journal of Personality and Social Psychology,* 70, 66–78.

Walton, R.E. and McKersie, R.B. (1991). *A Behavioural Theory of Labor Negotiations: An Analysis of a Social Interaction System.* 2nd edition. Ithaca, NY: Cornell University Press.

Weir, D.R. (2009). *The Way of Trance.* New York: Strategic Books.

Yukl, G. (2012). *Leadership in Organizations.* 8th edition. Harlow: Pearson

INDEX